Anthony Stafford

Life of the Blessed Virgin

Together With the Apology of the Author

Anthony Stafford

Life of the Blessed Virgin
Together With the Apology of the Author

ISBN/EAN: 9783337279028

Printed in Europe, USA, Canada, Australia, Japan

Cover: Foto ©Lupo / pixelio.de

More available books at **www.hansebooks.com**

THE FEMALL GLORY.

"Hail, *Solomon's Throne!*
Pure *Ark* of the Law!
Fair *Rainbow!* and *Bush*
Which the *Patriarch* saw!
Hail, *Gideon's Fleece!*
Hail, blossoming *Rod!*
Samson's Sweet *Honey Comb!*
Portal of God!"
                    Lyra Catholica.

"Hail, *Virginal Mother!*
Hail, Purity's *Cell!*
Fair *Shrine*, where the Trinity
Loveth to dwell!
Hail, *Garden* of Pleasure
Celestial *Balm!*
Cedar of Chastity!
Martyrdom's *Palm!*"
                    Lyra Catholica.

The Life of the Blessed Virgin;

TOGETHER WITH

THE APOLOGY OF THE AUTHOR,

Now *first* printed.

By ANTHONY STAFFORD.

A NEW EDITION,

With *Seven* Illustrations after *Overbeck*.

" Behold a Virgin shall conceive, and bear a SON."
ISAIAH.

LONDON:
Printed and published for a *Layman* of the *Scotch Church*, and sold by *Edward Lumley*,
514, New Oxford Street.
1860.

"How worthily is she honoured of men, whom the *Angel* proclaimed beloved of GOD! O *Blessed Mary!* he cannot bless thee, he cannot honour thee too much, that deifies thee not. That which the *Angel* said of thee thou hast prophesied of thyself; we believe the *Angel* and thee. All Generations shall call thee *Blessed*, by the FRUIT of whose Womb all generations are blessed."—BISHOP HALL.

"WE admit genuine, universal, Apostolic Traditions . . . the perpetual Virginity of the *Mother* of GOD."
ARCHBISHOP BRAMHALL.

"THE *Blessed Virgin Mother* is undoubtedly the most highly exalted and honoured of all creatures . . . . All generations, according as her Divine Canticle foretold, do call her *Blessed*. And certainly the highest honour that can be paid to a creature is due to her."
BISHOP JOLLY.

THE PREFACE TO THE NEW EDITION.

HIS PREFACE *Contains* :—

I. *All that has been discovered of the* Author *of* " The Femall Glory," *with some notice of his works from* Wood's " Athenæ Oxoniensis :"—

II. Henry Burton's *attack upon the Book, from his Sermon on* " Fear God ; honour the King ;" *for the delivery of which he was censured by the* Star Chamber :—

III. *The criticism of* W^m. Prynne, *from* Canterburies Doom :—

IV. *A few words of defence, from an Answer to* Burton *by* Peter Heylin ; *a work which was licensed by* Laud's Chaplain, *and written by his Command* :—

V. *An extract from a reply to* Burton's *Sermon, by* Christopher Dow: *And to these are added ;*—

Preface to the New Edition.

The Author's *Own* Apology *of his Work, dedicated to* Archbishop Laud *and* Bishop Juxon, *and now for the* first time *printed.*

One object *with which* " The Femall Glory " *is reprinted, is to show that a staunch member of the* English Church *has written a Life of* S. Mary, *of a* Catholic *type, which has commanded the approval of such eminent* Prelates *as* Laud *and* Juxon. *This, however, is the least important reason which determined the present reprint. There exists, it is believed, no Life of the* Blessed Virgin, *beyond mere sketches of the dryest and most meagre description. It is hoped, that to some extent, and to comparatively few persons,* " The Femall Glory" *will supply this deficiency. If it only suggests to others the possibility to produce another Life more suited, in some respects, to the age in which we live, either as a compilation or as an original work, sufficient benefit will be ensured from the publication. Meanwhile, we here possess, whatever be its merits, or its faults, a book of genuine* English *growth, unadapted from* Foreign *works, and identical with the original edition. Hence, it has a value of its own, which it will retain, even if superseded by another Life of more modern origin and mode of thought and expression. Whether or not the book will be appreciated by those for whose benefit it is reprinted, remains to be proved.*

It has been thought wise to reproduce much

Preface to the New Edition.

that was originally written against "The Femall Glory," in order to anticipate criticisms which may arise, in certain quarters, at the present day. All that can be said against the work has been said two centuries ago; so that, at the most, modern attacks will but repeat what has been previously urged. To these attacks have been added, amongst others, the Author's own Apology of his book; a reply which, perhaps, many will consider sufficiently complete. If not, Readers are requested to form their own independent judgment, on a candid perusal of the whole book. It is enough for some amongst us, at the present day, to remain content with the deliberate decision—on points of doctrine, not in matters of taste—of a Martyr who is only not a Saint, and of a Confessor who acted in the Spirit of a Martyr. Perhaps there are not many persons now living who are competent, either by parts or endurance, to place their opinion in opposition to the judgment of such men as Laud and Juxon. It would certainly become few to presume to defend that with which they were well satisfied.

The present reprint is a verbatim et literatim copy of the first edition of "The Femall Glory," and of the only MS. of the Apology known to be in existence, that, namely, in the Library of Queen's College, Oxford—with but two exceptions; one word has been altered in the Text, and a single letter in the Apology, neither variation being of any theological value. A copy of the Second Edition to which Wood refers has not been discovered.

I.

"*Anthony Stafford*, an *Esquire's* Son, was born of an ancient and noble family in *Northamptonshire*, being descended from those of his name living at *Blatherwicke*, in that *County*, entered a *Gentleman Commoner* of *Oriel College* in 1608, [*Wood* wrong here; *Stafford* matriculated *March* 8, 1604-5] and in that of his age 17, where by the help of a careful *Tutor*, but more by his natural parts, he obtained the name of a good scholar, and became well read in ancient History, Poets, and other Authors.

"What stay he made in that *House* I cannot yet tell, or whether he took the Degree of *B.A.* according to the usual course. Sure I am that in 1609 he was permitted to study in the Public Library, purposely to advance his learning, having then a design to publish certain matters; and in 1623, just after the *Act*, he was actually created *M.A.*, as a 'person 'adorned with all kinds of Literature.'

"His works are these:—

"NIOBE DISSOLVED INTO A NILUS: *or his Age drowned in her own tears*, &c. London, 1611.

Preface to the New Edition.

"MEDITATIONS AND RESOLUTIONS; *Moral, Divine, and Political, Cent. I.* London, 1612.

"HEAUENLY DOGGE: or *Life and Death of that Great Cynick*, Diogenes; *whom* Laertius *styles* Canis Cœlestis, *the Heavenly Dogge*, &c. London, 1615.

"THE GUIDE OF HONOUR: *or the balance where she may weigh her actions*, [written in foreign parts.] London, 1634.

"THE FEMALL GLORY: *or the Life of the* Blessed Virgin Mary. Printed at London with Cuts, 1635. This little book, pen'd in a flourishing stile, was in another impress entituled the PRECEDENT OF FEMALL PERFECTION: *or the Life of the Blessed Virgin Mary*. But the said book being esteemed egregiously scandalous among the *Puritans*, who looked upon it as purposely published to encourage the *Papists*, Henry Burton, *Minister* of Friday Street in *London*, did pretend to discover, in his Sermon entituled *For* GOD *and the King*, several extravagant and *Popish* passages therein; and advised the people to be aware of it. ' *For which and nothing else*, [as W^m. Prynne ' tells us in CANTERBURY DOOM] *he was* ' *brought into the* Star Chamber, *and there* ' *censured. But on the contrary, this* Popish

'Book of Stafford's (*as he calls it*), *with many*
'*scandalous passages in it, was, by the* Arch-
'bishop's *special direction, professedly justified,*
'*both by* Dr. Heylin, *in his* MODERATE ANSWER
'TO MR. BURTON, *and by* Christopher Dow,
'*in his* INNOVATIONS UNJUSTLY CHARGED:
'*and this Book neither called in, nor corrected,*
'*so audaciously* Popish *was he grown, in this*
'*particular amongst many others.*'

"A JUST APOLOGY: or *Vindication of a Book entituled* FEMAL GLORY, *from the false and malevolent aspersions cast upon it by* Henry Burton, *of late deservedly censured in the* Star Chamber. Whether this Book was ever published I know not: I once saw it in a 4to. *MS.* in the Library of *Dr. Thomas Barlow*, given to him by *Sir John Birkenhead*.

"HONOUR AND VERTUE TRIUMPHING OVER THE GRAVE: *Exemplified in a faire devout Life, and Death, adorned with the surviving perfections of* Henry Howard, Lord Stafford, *lately deceased; which Honour, in him, ended with as great a lustre as the Sunne sets in a serene sky,* &c. London, 1640.

"At the end of which are divers Elegies upon the death of the said *Lord*, most written by *Oxford* men, especially those of *S. John's College*. Our Author, *Anthony Stafford*, who was kinsman to said *Lord*, hath also translated from *Latin* into *English*, the ORATION OF JUSTUS

Preface to the New Edition.

Lipsius against Calumny. 1612. [This was printed at the end of his Meditations and Resolutions.]

" What other things he hath written, or tranflated I know not, nor anything elfe of him; only that he died, as I have been informed, in the time of the Civil Wars.

" [*Stafford's* Niobe, &c. given by *Wood* as the *firft* of that Author's Works, is only a continuation, or *fecond* part, of a Treatife which our biographer feems not to have been aware of. This is—

" Niobe: or *his Age of Tears; a Treatife no lefs profitable and comfortable, than the Times damnable: Wherein Death's Vizard is pulled off, and his Face difcovered not to be fo fearful as the Vulgar makes it; and withal, it is Shewed, that Death is only bad to the bad, good to the good.* London, 1611. Dedicated to *Robert Earl* of *Salifbury*, becaufe, fays the Author, my Father was a neighbour to your Father, being much obliged unto him, and my own family unto yourfelf.]"—Athenæ Oxoniensis, by *Anthony à Wood*, 4to. Ed. 1817: *Philip Blifs.*

II.

" Add wee hereunto another Booke, intituled The Femall Glory, by *Anthony Stafford*, printed by Authority, 1635, wherein he mightily Deifies the *Virgin Mary*, calling her the '*Grand White Immaculate* Abbeſſe *of your* '*ſnowy Nunneries,*' to whom he ſpeaks, and before whom he would have them to '*kneele* '*preſenting the* All-ſaving BABE.' Loe, hence a change of our GOD into a *Goddeſſe*. And theſe hee commends, '*the Sacred Arithmetic,* '*in praying on their beades.*' And he commends ' Candlemas Day, *for the lights burning* '*and Maſſe ſinging, taken from the* Heathen '*guiſe, and converted into* Chriſtian :' and '*that which was performed by ſuperſtitious* '*Idolaters in honour of* Ceres *and* Proſerpina '(Heathen Goddeſſes) *may be turned into the* '*prayſe and glory of the* Virgin Mary.' Again, '*this day is made holy by the Purification of the* '*Mother.*' The Aſſumption of his *Lady* is ſet forth with a picture, how ſhe is taken up into *Heaven*, with Verſes. Hee ſeems to hold the *Virgin Mary* to have beene without ſinne. Hee boldly beares himſelfe upon the '*approba-* '*tion of the* Church *of* England, *in magnifying* '*the* Virgin Mary, *not as a meere* Woman, *but as* '*a* Type *or* Idæa *of an accompliſht Piety.*' He calls her '*White Spotleſſe Sowle,*' and '*Purity* '*itſelfe.*' He ſpeaks in one place of her '*all-* '*holy heart,*' as in another, of our '*All-Holy-* '*LORD.*' He preferres the errour of the adoring extreame, before the *Puritans* neglecting of her, in calling her *Mal*, GODS *Mayd*, and rejecting *Hail*, Mary, *Full of Grace.* Again,

Preface to the New Edition.

hee faith, '*Of one thing I will assure them, till* '*they are good* Marians, *they shall never be good* '*Christians.*' Of sundry Grandees hee faith, '*All which are canonized for* Saints, *and have* '*erected and dedicated Temples to her memory.*' Hee recites the many Orders of the Sodalitye, styling them '*great, worthy, and pious people,*' and concludes thus :—'*For shame let not us* '*alone deny her that honour and praise which* '*all the world allowes her.*' And, '*my Arith-* '*metic will not serve mee to number all those who* '*have registered their names in the* Sodalitie *of* '*the* Rosary *of this our* Blessed Lady; *the ori-* '*ginal of which is derived from the Battaile of* '*Naupactun, gain'd by* John *of* Austria, *and* '*the* Christians; *which Victory was attributed* '*to her Intercession with her* Sonne.' Loe, here the *New Great Goddesse Diana* whom the whole *Pontifical* World worshippeth! He invocates her saying, '*O pardon, gracious* Prin-'cesse, *my weake endeavours to Summe up thy* '*value:*' '*Thou deserv'st a Quire of* Queens '*here, and another of* Angels *in* Heaven, *to* '*sing thy praises:*' '*I confesse, O my Sweetest* '*Lady! that now I have said all I can of thee,* '*I have but done like* Timanthes:' '*To give* '*thee an estimation answerable to thy merit, is a* '*thing impossible.*' Many more passages might be added. He calls her '*Womans dearest* Mis-'tresse,' '*a glorious* Empresse,' '*Empresse of* '*the lower world.*' Hee says of her, '*If* CHRIST '*was faire above the Sons of men, should not she* '*be so above their Daughters?*' And in the Epistle to the *Feminine Reader*, '*This is she,* '*who was on* Earth *a* Confirmer *of the good* '*and a* Reformer *of the reprobate,*' &c. And in the Epistle to the *Masculine Reader*, '*Truely* '*I beleeve that the undervaluing of* One *so great* '*and deare in* CHRIST'S *Esteeme, cannot but bee* '*displeasing to Him; and that the more we* '*ascribe to her, (setting Invocations apart)* '[Heere he contradicts his owne practise, O '*pardon gratious* Princesse] *the more gratious* '*we appear in His Sight.*' And he concludes it thus, '*I will onely adde this, that since the* '*finishing of this Story, I have reade a Booke of* '*the now* Bishop [Montacute] *of* Chichester, '*entituled* Apparatus, &c. *and am glad to finde* '*that I have not digressed from him in any one* '*particular.*' So hee. Loe, therefore, what a *Metamorphosis* of our *Religion*. Here is a *New Goddesse* brought in amongst us. The *Author* glorieth, '*that hee who is the* first *who hath* '*written* (as he saith), *in our vulgar tongue, on* '*the* Blessed Virgin;' and GOD grant hee be the last. But he leans himselfe in al this upon the *Church of England*—where I pray you? At last I perceive, that this *Church of England* is the now *Bishop* of *Chichester*, in his *Apparatus, &c.* '*from whom he hath not digressed in* '*any particular.*' And surely it were strange, that such a Mystery of Iniquity could be found but in a *Prelate*, and in this one by name, for a tryed Champion of *Rome*, and so, a *devout Votary to his* Queene *in* Heaven."—FOR GOD AND THE KING. *The Summe of two Sermons preached on the* fifth *of* November *last, in* St. Matthews, Friday Street, 1636. *By Henry Burton, Minister of* GODS *Word there and then.* 1 Pet. ii. 17. Fear GOD; Honour the *King*.

III.

" *Anthony Stafford* thus extolls, nay justifies the Invocation of the *Virgin*, and saying *Aves* to her :—

'*Tu gaudi Verbum peperisti & dicit* Avete Omnibus :'

(Meditationes, &c.)

He proceeds thus in the *Reverse* of the *Ghyrlond* :—

'*The* House *of God, the* Gate *of* Heavens *Power.*'

In the *Pannegyricke* :—

'*To whom the* Hierarchy *doth throng.*'

He styles her '*Most Excellent* Princesse,' 'Virgin Mother *of* GOD,' 'Empresse,' '*The alone Faire*,' '*Glorious* Empresse,' '*White Spotlesse* Soule,' '*Woman's Dearest* Mistresse,' '*Our Sweetest* Lady.' There is a picture [*in the original*] of her fabulous Assumption into *Heaven*, cut in brasse, after the *Popish* forme, with men and women devoutly kneeling and praying to her, and these verses written under the same:—

"What honor could to this great *Queene* be done,
  More then be taken up to *Heauen* high
  And there haue GOD for Father, Spouse, & Sonne,
  The *Angels* wayte, the world stand wondring by."

After which hee spends many pages to prove 'the verity [of *S. Mary's* Assumption, as an] 'undoubted truth.' Whereas indeed, it is a meere *Popish* ridiculous false Legend. And to prove this, he makes her to be borne without Sinne.

"This Booke of *Stafford's* giving very great scandall to *Protestants*, and encouragements to *Papists*, *Mr. H. Burton* in his Sermon, intituled 'For GOD *and the* King,' discovered and censured these extravagent *Popish* passages in it, advising the people to beware of it. For which, amongst other things, he was brought into the *Star Chamber*, and there censured. But on the contrary, this *Popish* Booke of *Stafford's* with the forementioned scandallous passages in it, were, by the *Archbishop's* special direction, professedly justified, both by *Dr. Heylin* in his 'BRIEFE AND MODERATE AN-'SWER,' (licensed by the *Archbishop's* owne *Chaplain*, and written by his command); and by *Christopher Dow*, in his 'INNOVATIONS UNJUSTLY CHARGED;' and this Booke neither called in, nor corrected.—So audaciously *Popish* was he growne, in this particular among many others."—CANTERBURIES DOOM: *or the first part of a Compleat History of the Commitment, Charge, Tryall, Condemnation, and Execution of* W^m. Laud, *late* Archbishop *of* Canterbury. *By* W^m. Prynne *of* Lincoln's Inn, *Esquire.*

IV.

"As for the Booke intituled THE FEMALE GLORIE, you find not in it, that I see by your [*Burton's*] Collections, any thing posatively or dogmatically delivered contrarie unto any point of Doctrine established and received in the *Church* of *England.* Some swelling language there is in it, and some *Apostrophes*, I perceive by you [*Burton*] to the *Virgin Marie*, which if you take for *Invocations* you mistake his [*Stafford's*] meaning; who tells us plainly, as you cite him, 'that the more we ascribe unto 'her, setting Invocation apart, *the more gracious* 'we appeare in our SAVIOURS Sight.' No innovation hitherto in point of Doctrine."—A BRIEF AND MODERATE ANSWER *to the Seditious and scandallous challenge of* Henry Burton, *late of* Friday Street, *in two Sermons by him preached, &c. By Peter Heylin.* 1637.

V.

"Neither have I seen that other Booke called THE FEMALL GLORY, nor will I spend words, by way either of censure or defence of it, upon fight only of thofe fragments which here hee [*Burton*] prefents us with, as well knowing his art, and at what rate to value his credit in quotations. Yet in all thofe panegyrick ftraines of *Rhetorick*, (for fuch for the moft part they feem, rather than pofitive affertions) he [*Stafford*] hath not deviated fo much to the one extreme, as *Mr. Burton's* Marginall hath to the other, in fcoffingly calling the *New Great Goddeffe Diana*. And if it be true, that hee [*Stafford*] hath not digreffed, in any particular, from [*Montacute*] the *Bifhop* of *Chichefter*, as *Mr. Burton* makes him affirm; I dare boldly fay *Mr. Burton* will never be able to find the leaft point of Popery in it. For, it is well known, that *Bifhop* (to whom— as if hee had bid adieu to all civility, yea and fhame too—terms a *Tried Champion of* Rome, and fo, *a Devout Votary to the* Queene *of* Heaven) hath approved himfelf fuch a *Champion* againft *Rome* that they that have tried his ftrength, durft never yet come to a *fecond* encounter."—INNOVATIONS UNJUSTLY CHARGED UPON THE PRESENT CHURCH AND STATE: or an *Anfwer to the moft materiall paffages of a libellous Pamphlet, made by* Mr. Henry Burton, *and intituled,* An Apologie of an Appeale. *By* Chriftopher Dow, *B.D.* 1637.

Vigil of S. James.
A. D. 1860.

Ἀιὲν Ἀριστεύειν.

A Just Apology

OR,

A Vindication of a Booke entituled
THE FEMALE GLORY,

From ye falſe and malevolent Aſperſions caſt uppon it by Henry Burton, *of late deſervedly cenſured by ye Starr Chamber.*

"Hail! Thou that art highly favoured.
BLESSED art Thou among Women."—S. GABRIEL.

"BLESSED art thou among Women."—S. ELIZABETH.

"All generations ſhall call me BLESSED."—S. MARY.

Dedicated to

The moſt Reverend Father in GOD, *William,*
Lord Arch-Biſhoppe of *Canterbury,* His Grace;
And *William,* Lord Biſhoppe of *London,* and Lord Treaſurer of *England;*

His moſt honour'd & ſingular good Lords,

By

ANTHONY STAFFORD, Gent.

"If any one does not confefs that . . . . the *Holy Virgin* is the *Mother* of God, ... let him be *Anathema*."—Council of Ephesus.

"Then faid the Lord unto me: This *Gate* fhall be fhut, It fhall not be opened, and no man fhall enter in by It; becaufe the Lord, the God of *Ifrael* hath entered in by It, therefore It fhall be fhut."
Ezekiel xliv. 2.

MY MOST HONNOURED LORDES;

Y Soule is divided betweene an humble defire to importune your *Lordſhips* with lines unworthy your peruſall, and a reverend feare leaſt I ſhould interrupt your more ſerious thoughts, & your great important affaires. But, my Gracious *Lordes*, neceſſity (an obſerver of neither lawes, nor Holy-daies) commands, & I muſt obey; and (though wth the breach of good manners) endeavour to keepe my Faith unſuſpected. With bended Knees I dayly beſeech GOD, that I may dye according to that of *Tacitus,* " *bona fama, potius quam magna.*" Yet, is not my Reputation ſo deare to mee, that I will not forgive all injuries done mee, either in Fame, or in Fortune, with the ſame facility they are acted. My Mynd is of proofe againſt all theſe; for I have learned in my SAVIOUR's Schoole to endure all wronges of this Nature; but hee that calls my Religion

Tacitus.

in queſtion, & bringes my Faith to GOD in ſuſpition, toucheth me to the quicke, & gives me a deepe wound, w[ch] hee can never heale, ſo that the ſcarre will not remaine. Hee that is not tender and ſenſible this way, unmanneth himſelfe, & is at but beſt a Monſter of Nature in humane ſhape. By Religion, my Soule is joind, and marrydd, to her Maker & Redeemer; & hee that maliciouſly and falſly publiſheth a divorce betweene GOD and her, is by farre more cruell than hee, who, by violence, ſeparates her from the body ſhe hath ſo long inhabited; her vnion with the latter being not ſo ſtrong, as that with the former. This deadly blow I have received, my moſt *Reverend Lordes*, for I am brought upon the ſtage by the *Firſt borne of Infamie*, one *Burton*, heretofore a ſweep[r] of his Ma[ties] Cloſett, for an Innovatour; for a Blaſphemer of my Heavenly FATHER; & a baſe Deſertour of my Mother *Church*, from whoſe Holy Breſts I never ſuckt any corrupt Nouriſhment.

H. Burton.

Hee ſays I have, "*in a Booke intituled* THE "FEMALE GLORY, *Deified a Creature, the* Holy Virgin Mary, *&* *made her equall to her* CREATOUR." Though this abominable vntruth will appeare to any man of comon ſenſe, who ſhall reade that Treatyſe of myne; yet are there ſo many, who will never peruſe it, but will take all Allegations brought againſt mee, by my

H. Burton's *Sermon: For* GOD *&* *the* King.

malevolent Adversary, for true, that I shall never be able to wipe off the scandall. Once I determined to answeare his Forgeries; but that thought left me, when I understoode from *Doctor Heylins Reply* to this simple Schismatique, that your *Lordships*, and the *Church*, were resolved to vouchsafe, neither him, nor any of his fellow-fooles any further *Answer*; but that they should henceforward write at y° perill of their ears. Being in this perplexity, not knowing what course to take, I consulted with my best, and most knowing Friends, who unanimously advised mee not to penne any publique Satisfaction, for *two* reasons; the *first* was, for that yo[r] *Lordships* had forbidden it; the *next*, that those obstinate spirits that would not reade my former *Booke*, would much lesse surveigh my ensuing *Defence*. Yet, did they judge it most fitt, that I should endeavour to give your *Lordships* satisfaction, because to you both I owe it; & lest I should incurre your ill opinions, a disaster w[ch] I would not willingly outlive. To you, my *Lordes Grace*, I stand obliged to lay my Bosome open, in that I have dependency on your *Grace*; you being the most *Honnourable Lord* & *Chancellour* of this *Vniversity*, whereof I glory to be a Member. To you, my *Lord of London*, I am ingaged further to expresse myselfe, because by your Authority my *Booke* was licenc'd; & consequently, no disgrace can light on mee without reflecting on yõ. And to make this short *Apologie*, another Motive, and a continuall Remembrancer, is the honnour and happinesse I have, to bee often conversant with the learned & prudent *President*, & *Fellowes*, of that *Colledge* wch will for ever glory in both your Governments, & predicate yor Bounty by wch it hath beene so much beautified, and inlarged. I know yor *Lordshipps* love frugality in wordes, I will therefore onely use so^e many as shall both give you an account, why I presum'd to put my Sickle into the Divines Harvest in wryting this *Booke*; & also free mee from the odious Aspersions of the *Spirituall Rebell*; & vindicate the *Booke* itselfe frõ the venemous slanders laide on it. The Labour will not bee great; for the meere quoting of diverse places in it, wch directly make against the profane Idolatrizing of this Superlative Saint, will iustifie me in all eyes, but in those of envy, and her brood.

As for the *first*, being by many tyes obliged to a most vertuous & learned Lady of this Land, I conceived I could present her with nothing more acceptable, in her sight, than the Lives OF THE FEMALE SAINTS, which were never yet, by any man, truly & elegantly written. And to begin this Worke with THE BLESSED VIRGIN, the comõn method of others, Piety, & my Conscience, enioined mee. True

A Just Apology.

it is, I have never received Holy Orders; but as true I ever aspired to that great Dignity; & of all Studies was ever most delighted with that of Divinity. More over, this being but a History, I saw the penning of it required no subtilty at all, but onely iudgment & language; in w^{ch}, though I bee no Master, I am no Apprentice; & my affectionate Zeale to the Story, made me confident I should reape (if no Honour) no shame in composing it.

NOW TOUCHING MY BOOKE.

In my Epistle to the Read^r, I make a Protestation in these formall wordes :— "*Yet wthall*
"*I professe that I am her Admirer, not Idolater,*
"*and that I no way allow of their profane Cus-*
"*tome, who rob* GOD *of His Honour, and be-*
"*stowe it on her. But this I will say, that*
"*though I impute not the late troubles and af-*
"*flictions of the* Protestant Partie *in Germany,*
"*to the small Reverence these paid her*, ('many
" 'of GOD's Judgments,' *according to* St Augus-
" tine, ' being secret, none uniust') *yet truly I*
"*beleeve, that the undervaluing of* One *so great*
"*and deare in* CHRISTS *Esteeme, cannot but be*
"*displeasing to Him, & that the more wee*
"*ascribe to her* (setting Invocation apart) *the*
"*more gracious we appeare in His Sight.*"

Againe in my *Pannegericke,* I say thus :—
" *Thus* Holy Virgin *have I shaddowed o're*

Femall Glory: To the Masculine Reader.

A Pannegyricke upon the Blessed Virgin.

> "Thy Picture, in a rude unpolished score,
> "That wisht t'have drawne it, wth as lively Grace
> "As ever Painter drew the sweetest Face;
> "Yet, would I not idolatrize thy Worth,
> "Like some whose superstition sets thee forth,
> "In costly Ornaments, in Cloths so gay,
> "So rich, as never in the Stable lay,
> "Theese make thy Statues now as famous bee,
> "For pride, as thou wert, for Humility.
> "I cannot thinke thy Virgin-Bashfullnesse
> "Would weare the Lady of Loretto's Dresse,
> "Though farre more glorious Robes to thee were give^n,
> "Meeknesse, & Zeale on earth, Glory in Heaven.
> "Take then the Honour thou hast iustly wonn,
> "Praise aboue Angells, but below thy SONN."

In another part of my Booke, I thus farther declare, how much I abhorre the Idolatry wth wch I am so uniustly charged :—

Life of the Blessed Virgin: Her Internall Beauty.

> "Here my Invention treads a Maze, and my
> "heart is divided betweene an earnest desire to
> "praise her to the height, and an holy feare,
> "least in that Praise I should trench on GOD's
> "Owne peculiar Attributes. That she was no
> "way inferiour to her SONNE according to the
> "Flesh, I dare not with some avouch, who mag-
> "nifie her in a phrase that violates her Mo-
> "desty, and makes her to blush at her owne Ex-

A Just Apology.

"altation. Her Lowlinesse was such, that it
"was neerer the reiecting of all Commendations,
"then entertaining a comparison, betweene her
"selfe, and Him to Whom she had professed her-
"selfe a Handmaiden. And no lesse is her shame,
"or indeed her trembling, when pens profanely
"prodigall, ascribe that Honour to her, wch is
"onely proper and due to that DEITY, from w^{ch}
"she received her Grace, and Being. I will not
"wth Lipsius ascribe as much to her Milke, as to   Lipsius.
"her SONNE'S BLOOD ; neither dare I side with
"those who averre that she was halfe of that Sacri-
"fice that ransom'd us, and GOD'S Partner heere.
"Nor is my penne so impiously valiant, as to ius-
"tifie that GOD made Himselfe the Patterne, and
"communicated to her by Grace whatsoever Hee
"had by Nature. Nor am I of his bold Opinion,
"who saies, if man had never sinned, yet CHRIST
"should have taken Flesh, to honour her. These
"men would have her in all things equall to
"CHRIST Him Selfe. Neither her Modesty,
"nor myne, will admit of this blasphemous flat-
"tery. I willingly allow her to bee the Vessell,
"but not the Fountaine of Grace. I am much
"taken with his Tenet who auers that GOD
"made all things for the use of man, because He
"would amply furnish him wth matter enough to
"busy his head, least hee should be so audacious
"as to enquire into His Secrets, and encroach
"upon His Prerogatives. Wee need not (thanks

"to His infinite Goodneſſe) bee ſo dangerouſly venturous, ſince He affordes vs large ſcope and ground enough ſafely to extoll this His Favorite, ſecond *to none that ever bore Fleſh, either in her owne Deſert, or in His Eſteeme.*"

Alſo in another place, I ſhow my conformity, and reverence to the *Church of England* in this very forme:—

"Wherefore I moſt humbly ſubmitt this, and all things elſe Divine by mee handled, to the cenſure and determination of the Church of England, *whoſe not Connivence alone, but Approbation I know I ſhall have, in boldly affirming that ſhe was a tranſcendent* Creature, *not to be ranck't, in reſpect of her Worth, with any of her Sexe, but to have a place aſſign'd her apart and above them all, &c."*

Would a man think that Malice and her ſpawne, after the reading of this my naked, and open Profeſſion could find any thing to carpe at? Yet, they doe; and make mee ſeeme, in many points, blamable. Their *firſt*, and maine, quarrell is againſt the Picture of her, in the [*original*] Frontiſpiece, wch is as terrible to them as a Lanſcippe with a May-pole in it. Sure I am, I have ſeene her Images hung up in moſt of the *Lutheran Churches* in *Chriſtendome*, wch may take this ſcruple out of their myndes; for certainly wee owe more to *Luther*, for the Reformation of our *Church*, than to *Calvin*; the

---

Life of the Bleſſed Virgin: *Her Aſſumption.*

one being a Planter, the other but a Pruner, though I will not deny him to have beene a man of moſt excellent partes. This I find, by experience, that by often ſeeing her Portrait, & that of her Deareſt Sonne, I many tymes recall Him & His Merits, her & her Perfections, to my mynd, wch before was void of ſuch Heavenly Gueſts. For whatſoever invigitates the eye, leaves a ſtronger impreſſion in the Soule, then that wch onely pierceth the Eare; wch Truth, hee ſhall eaſily diſcover, who ſhall firſt heare a Hiſtory only reade, & after ſee it acted on the Theatre. When, & wherever I ſee her Semblance, then, & there I pay a Reverence to the lovely Vnion of all thoſe rare Vertues, of wch ſhe is the happy Miſtreſſe; but it is not the ſame Reverence I render her Maker, and myne. To adore this meekeſt of women, who would loath both the Adoration, & the Adorer, were (according to the old Adage) "*veneri immolare ſuem.*" This is the utmoſt Divine vſe wee, of the *Engliſh Church*, make of her Figure. For if wee deny Veneration to thoſe glorious Heavenly Bodies, certainly we ſhall not give it to wood, and colors. For my owne part, I ſeriouſly vowe that did I live und'r a *Prince* as impious, and tyrranous, as myne is Pious, and Merciful; & that this Monſter were ſuch an *Anti-Marian* that hee rewarded the leaſt civill reſpect done her, wth moſt hideous Tortures, and abhorred Deaths, I would, on his Racks & amidſt his Flames, confeſſe how much, and how deſervedly, I honour her; but not to ſuch a height, as to diſhonour her LORD and SAVIOUR. Yet, ſhould I give her that Worſhip I onely owe to GOD, & kneele to her till my knees turn'd brawne, my offence ſurely would not be ſo great, as if I ſhould wth *Burton* call her the *Great Goddeſſe Diana*, a ſinne directly againſt the Maieſty of the Sacred SONNE, in likening His Bleſſed *Mother* to a vaine, fictitious *Goddeſſe*. I think he doubts as much of the ſtory of the one, as of ye other. Sure I am, his deteſtable aſſertion infers as much. Of one thing I will aſſure him, that as there is not a greater argument, that there is plenty of fooles, then that hee, and his companions in ignorance can finde means how to live; ſo there is not a more evident proofe that this *State* is not *Popiſhly* affected, then y^t it ſuffers him to breathe a minute longer. For had hee vented this blaſphemy in any *Country* where the *Romiſh Religion* is profeſſed, hee, and his *Booke*, had ere this beene conſumed in fire; or, at leaſt, hee had beene hanged with it about his necke.

To ſhow how much hee vnd^r values her, hee rails at mee for ſaying "*that* (ſetting In-"vocation apart) *the more wee honour her, the* "*more gracious wee appeare in our* SAVIOURS

H. Burton's Sermon.

Femall Glory: To the Maſculine Reader.

A Just Apology.

"*Sight:*" An assertion wch no good and sober *Christian* would dare to oppose. I call Truth to witnesse wth mee, that this is ye very place wch a *Romish Priest* exclaimed at, as violently as hee, though in a more mannerly invective: By wch all men of vnderstanding may clearly discerne how *Popish* was that Assertion of myne. This will I make good, that I have publish't no more in Praise of this Glorious *Virgin*, then one of his owne Profession hath printed in Commendation of his owne Wife, to whome hee gives the Epithite of *Excellent*; and avoucheth her to bee as perfect a Creature as Mortality can boast of, deriving her by a long Pedigree from *Foxes' Martyrs*. Yet, doe I not averre, that hee hath Deified her; for I confesse, shee would have made a very sorry *Goddesse*; I should have said a shrewish^d, for I thinke she excells *Juno* herselfe in wrath and jealousie. I see no reason why *Burton* should bee angry that I should find out as many perfections in GOD's Owne *Mother*, as hee, or any of his sottish brethren, can espy in any of their purest wives, when the eggs of their eies are at the highest elevation.

And this nameing her the *Mother* of GOD is another maine exception they make against me. I have already told them in my *Booke*, that the Vnion of both Naturs, GOD and Man, being in CHRIST, she must, by strong consequence, bring forth both GOD, and Man. But *Burton*, & his silly Fraternity, have not braines of a temper fine enough to distinguish betweene the *Mother* of GOD, and the *Mother* of the GODHEAD; the *first* of which shee truly is, the *latt'r* shee is not. Neither have they schollorship enough to finde a difference betweene an Apostrophe, and an Invocation. I am confident, I have, by this, sufficiently manifested to all good and iust *Readers*, that I have not Deified the *Holy Virgin;* but have manifestly proved the Proverb true, " *that a* Puritan *is like a Clocke,* w^{ch} *will* " *never sweare, but lye often.*"

I must now adde something in defense of my Style, wch hee so much inveighs at. Hee vehemently braies out against my Rhetoricall flowers, and my "*swelling language*" (as hee calls it). And this I nothing marvail at; for anything red not more enrageth a Turkey-Cocke, then Oratory incenceth him, & his Confederates. I know not whence they should sucke this detestation of all Humane Learning, but from the *Turkes.* They hold it most profane to mixe Humanity wth Divinity; and will not allow *Sarah* an Handmaid, a *Hagar*, to waite upon her. Truly, I can alleadge no surer cause of their wrangling and scolding, then their being destitute of theise humane helpes, this skill in the Artes and Sciences; for it is an vsuall course wth those who have no weapons

A Juſt Apology.

to defend themſelves, to runne afarre of, and rayle. I hope my language ſwells wth matter, not wth wind and froth, as theirs does. Nothing, in this world, is ſo irkeſome to me, as to heare their cold Opium Sermons, wch infuſe ſleepe inſtead of Knowledge into the heads of their Auditours. The *State* ſhould doe well, to ſend them to convert the *Indians*; for though theiſe wilde *People* vnderſtand them not, yet would they bee much taken with the dinne they make, as being more capable of noiſe then Reaſon. Can Patience it ſelfe (wth out being tired) indure their tedious pumping for improper phraſes? They ſeldome, or never, pen anything wch wee may perceivee by their being in ſuch paine and travaile for a ſupply of wordes; not vnlike a dull Poet of my Acquaintance, who ſweat ſo with labour to find out an Epithite, that he was fain to put of his Doublett. They preach often, read little; not unlike him that paſſeth more then he drinkes. They reade Authours; &, with much adoe, make a Collection of the ſcurffe and dandriffe of ſpeech. Certeynly they have invented many pretty wordes; the only pitty is, that they ſignifie nothing.

Their Prayers are ſutable to their Preaching, full of Battologies, and Tautologies. They call it, praying by the SPIRITT; but GOD forbid, that I ſhould ever beleeve that the HOLY

Ghost can dictate nonsense, & blasphemy against Himselfe; wch surely bolts out from them against their wills, for want of premeditation. I heard one of them pray for *King Iames*, of famous Memory, being then sicke at *Thebalds*, in these very wordes:—" Lord, " make Thou his Bed in tyme of his sicknesse; & " grant hee may raigne over vs, as long as the " Sunne & Moone endureth; and the Prince, " his Sonne, after him." Who is so dull as not to apprehend that (if God had heard his Prayer) the faire sereous *Prince* wee are now blest in, must have consequently have been the *Prince* of *Darknesse*; the day and night being deprived of theise two radiant Lights? Nay, more, the Vniverse it selfe must have come to ruine; such a dependance it hath on the Vertue of theise two Planetts. Wee speake not to *Princes* w^thout great study, and precogitancy; much lesse should wee to God, since an Age bestowed in contemplation cannot furnish us with wordes sutable to so Infinite a Worth, to so Glorious a Maiesty. God so willing eccept my ejaculatory Prayrs; al my others shal bee sett; for I can never thinke any wordes good enough for Goodnesse It Selfe. And were not theise men the sworne slaves of obstinacy, their obdurate hearts would be ravish't wth the Collects composed by the *Church* of *England*; it being the most perfect forme of Prayer, any

A Puritan's Prayer.

Church of the *Christian Worlde* can produce. I have reade it both in *Italian*, & *French*; and can assure them that the most able men of both theise *Nations* have it in admiration. Yet, theise Novellists (who disclayme all Antiquity, and condemne, in all things, the practise of y^e *Primitive Church*) abhorre, and sleight these Divine Collects, as much as they doe an obscene Ballad.

Theise men have ever Nature betweene their teeth, and torment her with repining, not so much at their owne harme, as the good of others. They have neither actuall, nor verball Charity: not actuall, for they relieve no man; not verball, for they censure all men. If there bee but *one* spott in a faire life, they fixe their eyes on that, and shut them against the beautifull remainder: not unlike to him, who looking onely on the Sunne's Eclipses, should iudge him darke and obscure; or by the onely viewe of the lees, despise the Wine. They leave the safe and ready Roade, and take By-waies of their owne, wch leade to dangerous Precipices, as faction, and combination against the *Church*, and *Common-Wealth*. They deprave GOD's Holy Orders of *Arch-Bishops*, *Bishops*, *&c*. They seeke to rob Him of His Altars, and barre Him Harmony in His Owne House. But it is nothing at all strange to mee, that they will not afford Him Altars, nor bowe before them, when they will not bend their knees at His SONNE's Name; nor ſtoope to His Anointed; nor to thoſe who, by Him, are placed over them, not as perpendicul^r Stones (as they falſely imagine) to braine or bruiſe them, but as holy Tapers to give them Light. That they deny the LORD the Melody wch Hee requires in His *Church* is apparent; for *Aſtolpho*, his horne, in *Orlando* affrighted not more all that heard it, then the ſound of an Organ terrifies them. One of their little learned Society not long ſince, declaymed bitterly againſt this Inſtrument, in ye Pulpit, ſaying " *that "though all men well knew, y^t the Divell was "made the Organ to tempt Eve, yet there were "found men ſo deſperatly wicked as to play vpõ "Organs.*" S^t. *Auſtin* (if they ſcorne not his Inſtructiõ), will tell them : — " *Muſicam ideo "approbari in Eccleſiâ, vt per oblectamenta au-"rium infirmior animus in aſcenſum pietatis aſ-"ſurgat.*" But what talke I of S^t *Auſtin* to them who revile the *Fathers*, and hold their beſt Doctrines and Sentences, but as Pearles gathered out of Mud. They are very angry wth theiſe *Holy Men*, becauſe they write not to the Meridian of their vnd^{r}ſtanding, as not vouchſafing to deſcend to their capacities. Sure I am had they ſupplyed the roomes of theſe grave *Fathers*, againſt the *Pelagians*, *Donatiſts*, and other Subtle Combatans, that then on all

A Puritan's Sermon.

S. Austin.

A Juſt Apology.

ſides aſſayl'd, the *Church*, I will not ſay Shee had beene defaced, (for ſo great a miſcheife GOD's Providence would not ſuffer) but ſhe had vndoubtedly endured as many diſgraces as afflictions, & had not enlarged her ſelfe, and flouriſhed, as at this day ſhee does. *Cicero* ſays of a *Romane* Dunce, in his tyme, "*that he would have beene a learned man amongſt the Brittains;*" & I will affirme that theiſe formall Hypocrits would have ſeem'd very profound had they lived in the *ninth* Age of the *Church*, when ignorance had ſo clouded her, that ſhee could ſcarſely ſee, or bee ſeene. They put mee in mynd of the *Chriſtians* w^{ch} *Lucian* ſpeakes of in the Life of *Peregrinus*, whom hee maintaines to have beene ſo ſimple that they would ent'taine any halfe learn'd Jmpoſtor, and afford him an eminent place amongſt them. This Atheiſt who ieered his owne Gods, noe doubt would not ſpare ours, nor thoſe His Servants who bore His Name, & therefore ſlanderoufly, queſtionleſſe, layd this imputation on them. But I will boldly, becauſe truely, affirme, that theiſe *Puritanicall Chriſtians* will admit of any *Church-Mountebanke*, any *Literator*, fo^e hee can ſhew him ſelfe ſeditious enough. Diſobedience to their *Sovereigne*, and his Edicts is a thing they p^rfeſſe. Hee commands to wearre the Surplice, and to reade his *Booke*, wch tollerates lawfull Recreations, on the Sab-

Cicero.

Lucian.

baoth, to the Congregations comitted to their charge. Moſt of them proteſt they had rather put of corruption, then put it on; that is, they had rather dye, then weare the one, or reade the other. Some more Politique amongſt them then the reſt, being driven to that ſtreight, that they muſt either bee conformable, or looſe their Livings, condeſcend to weare the Surplice; & to iuſtifie this their faƈt, vnder the coulor of Conformity, make this *Embleme* of *Innocency* more odious to the people, telling them that they would wear a Bable in yᵉ *Church* rather then leave GOD's Service, and diſobey their *King;* what elſe implying that the Surplice, and a Bable, are things equivalent. And one of them, not long ſince, ſeeing that hee muſt either publiquely reade the *Booke* of *Lawful Liberty,* or forgoe his Parſonage, deigns ſo to reade it, indeed, but wᵗʰ preface:—" *Beloved in* " *the* LORD, *I am commanded by my* Sovereigne " King Charles *to reade this Booke to you; but* " Queene Elizabeth *was a very wiſe and godly* " *Woman.*" Had I a deſire to write what hereby hee intimates, I could not doe it; an awful Reverence to GOD's *Vice-Gerent,* would ſo ſhake my hand. I muſt take leave ſo to certify them, that I have lived *two yeares* in their mother *Church* of *Geneva,* & that there is in their vſuall cuſtome, from after Dinner till Sermon tyme, & againe, from after Sermon till

A Puritan's Preface.

A Just Apology.

Night, to play at *Bowles, Nine-Pinns, Palle-Malle,* a *Game* they so calle, & to shoote in *Gunns,* & *Crosse-Bowes,* & to vse diverse other *Recreations.* But our Factionists think they doe nothing, if they excell not their Patterne, & therefore some of them wash their Handes & Faces, after the manner of Children, on Saturday at Night; some then cooke their Meate for Sunday; & others lye in their Cloths all night, because they will not dresse them selves on the Sabbaoth. Nay, I knowe not who shutt vp his Bees, and smothered them, because they should not worke on that day.

If your *Lordships* and the other *Bishops* should introduce the Wafer into y^e *Church* (wth wch the *Genevians* have received ever since their *first* Reformation, till within these few *years* past) what Combustion would they make in all the Quarters of this *Land?* Yet, hath the continuall vse of It not caused any, ye least Mutiny, or Insurrection, in that Citty.

Yet if theise men were onely thus ridiculous, they would make vs the better sport, & they might be connived at; but they are dangerous, even above the Jesuite. They teach Deposition of *Kings,* as *Dr. Owen,* in a *Booke* of his called Herod *and* Pilate *reconciled,* plainly demonstrates. Nay I had an *English Booke* of theirs, & thinke I can yet recover it, that vrgeth many Textes of Scripture, to prove the lawfull-

Dr. Owen's "Herod *and* Pilate *reconciled.*"

nesse, not onely of deposing, but also of murthering *Princes*, & quite puts downe *Mariana*, in that *King*-killing Doctrine. It was so contagious, that I was affraide it would have infected my other *Bookes*, & therfore I expell'd it my Study. They hold that yᵉ inferior Magistrate may depose the Superiour; & I remember to have reade a *Question*, put by one of theise Incendiaries:—" *Whether, or no, if the Head* " *bee giddy, the Handes may not lawfully bind* " *it?*" And they have a Prophecy as pernicious as this Question, wᶜʰ is:—" *That there* " *will never bee an Order in this Lland, till* " *there bee a Disorder;*" the dangerous Inference whereof is easy to bee vnderstood.

In what Esteem they have *Kinges*, is manifest to all men, by *Burton's* execrable and vnpardonable slander against *King Iames*, concerning the forementioned *Booke of Liberty*; wᶜʰ villanous scandall required his Head, as well as his Eares. This irreverence, and incivility, to *Princes* I imagine they might vnhappily drawe from *Luther*, who shakes up *Henry* 8. in a very vnmannerly style, calling him " *momum, mimum, stultum, Pharaonem;*" & all his Courtiers, hee termes " *Iannes, & Iambres.*" Hence wee learne at what an infamous rate this magnanimous *Prince* bought his *Tytle* of *Defender of the Faith*; for bye his *Booke* against *Luther* hee purchased it. I dare say, never

---

A Puritan's Question.

A Puritan's Prophecy.

H. Burton.

A Just Apology.

Prince & *Church-man* were better matcht then theise *two*. Though *Henry the* 8. was so fierce, & couragious that hee was called the *Man-Queller*, yet hee mett wth one of as fiery a temper as him selfe: For *Luther* had, as often as hee, fac'd danger, and death it selfe, though not the same way; his Valour beeing passive, the *King's* active. Yet, will the greatest Favourers of *Luther* acknowledge, that hee never gave a more barbarous Testimony of his high mynd, then hee did in so shamefully reviling this mighty *Monarch*. Hee might have learned from *Pliny* that, " *Eloquentia sine moribus male discitur.*" [Pliny.]

I have read that one of the *Christian Cæsars* making a publique Oration before a whole *Acadamie*, where in hee now and then stumbled. *Priscian*, a *Bishop*, standing behind him, said, in somwhat too lowd a whisper:—" Cæsar, *you have forgotten your Grammer.*" To whom, hee, as lowd, replied:—" Bishop, *you have forgotten your Ethickes.*" [Bishop.] [Cæsar.] Certainly, wee owe Reverence & Respect to the Dignity of *Princes*, though our enemies; much more are wee bound to pay it those who may rightly challenge the payment of that due Debt, by being placed by GOD over vs. Yet, as I said before, theise Reforming Mutineers make as bold wth the *King's Maiesty*, as they doe wth the *Pope's Holinesse*. How they have abused *King Iames*, I have already related; and can, wth the same facility, expose to open view, how much, & how often, they have iniured his *Heroicke Sonne* now reigning, a *Prince*, great in the Vnion of the *Roses*, greater in that of the *Lawrells*, but greatest of all, in the *Love* of his *People*. He knowes full well, that full ill it went with Mankind, if the Almighty MAKER of all thinges should confine His Favour to one, & neglect the remainder of Humanity, and therefore as a GOD on earth, (in imitatiõ of the Heavenly) distributes his Favours amongst his Subjects; but not *eodem gradu*, becaufe they are not *eiufdem meriti*. Like the Sunne, hee strives to impart the Light of his Countenance to all, and where his Beames cannot reach, thither his Warmth extends. Though all cannot enjoy the honour of his Prefence, all are sharers in the comforts of his Benefits. Hee hath beene, by his prudent Parent taught, that as a child that is hungry may bee still'd awhile wth dandling, and singing, but it must have the Breast, or it will not be contented long; so good and gracious wordes pleafe well, but good deeds (as doing iustice, and seeking the common good) are they wch give the chiefe content to subiects. Nor doth the care hee takes for vs ever weary him; but is as indefaticable in doing good as Heaven in motion. How fortunate are wee in living vnder such a *Prince*, who so farre excells his subiects in Vertue, as in Dignity. But more

A Just Apology.

happy are you, my *Gracious Lordes*, on whom his Beames are most plentifully bestowed; & no lesse blessed is hee in such *Counsell^{rs}*, in whom all the abilities of compleat Statists, & all the requisites of pious, & learned *Church-Men* conspire to advance the state of the *Church*, & *Common-Wealth*, wherein wee live; & by whose holy and sage monitions, our deare *Master's* Perfections are dayly both increased, and confirmed. O may Envy, wth all her Engines, never give a stopp to those your incessant endeavours to plant Peace & Plenty amongst us. Well may Malice pry into your Actions; but once I am sure shee shall never bee able to espie the least blemish in them. In yor Judicaturs, Impartiality holdes the Scales; & you imagine the Bench to bee your Death-Bed. From your afflicted Petitioners, you take not so° much as *Xeniola* (as *Pliny* professed of him selfe) and all the Fraudlesse *Iudges* the Auncients drewe, who tooke nothing frõ those, for whom they had done most; but held the Service of the *State* amply rewarded in it selfe. It is not vnknown to you, that the iust man is like the Fable of the Snake, who, though Death cut him in sunder, hee will ioine againe. Bee constant, most pious *Lordes*, in the vertuous, though rough and spiny course you are to runne; and approve your selves to bee the wise men *Senneca* speakes of, the state of whose mynd is

[marginal notes: Pliny. Senneca.]

like that of yᵉ world above the Moone, where there is no change. This doing, though Oblivion may seize on your Tombes, on yoʳ Etʳnall glorious Memories it shall not.

Having satisfied your owne Consciences, and the expectations of all good men, despise the vicious, & their Censures; for you owe neither the Divell, nor his Membʳˢ, any satisfaction.

I heare theise Enemies of GOD, and His *Church*, daily exclaime against your cruelty, & yet doubt of your Integritie in Religion, though you my *Lordes Grace* have publiquely expressed your Zeale to GOD, and His House wᵗʰ that Ardency, Ingenuity, and Affection, that a man would thinke you strove to demonstrate the Soule may bee made visible. They spare not to say, (to use their owne sordid style) "*that a cruell Counsellour to a Prince is yᵉ Hangman's Factour;*" & I will not forbeare to acquaint them wᵗʰ this Truth, "*that hee who is mercifull to yᵉ wicked, is cruell to the good.*" These *Zoili*, as at first their disabilities made them looke for no good from this *Church*, wherein Desert meets with its reward above its wish; so ever since by their private practises against her, they give a sure evidence they feare no evill shee can inflict. "*No Spirits* (saith *Livy*) *are so ready to envy, and malice others, as they whose Degree and Estate is not answerable to*

A Puritan's Proverb.

A Christianman's Reply.

Livy.

A Just Apology.

"their haughty *Myndes*; & such commonly, as they hate the *Vertue*, so they despise, the good *Fame of another*." How accursed and miserable were wee, if your *Lordshipps* were of a Disposition to entertaine the malice, and spite of such Detractours, & to interest, and insert publique Authority wth in their private Factions. Surely, such a slaughter of *English* would ensue, that we should swimme to our Temples in a Flood of our owne Bloods, & come backe by the same Streame. But (thankes bee to GOD) your *Lordships*, & the rest of that *Honourable Court* are soe farre from hearkening to their idle libellous suggestions, that you have chastised the Authours of them, though farr below the merit of their crimes. "*Acerrimus emendator timor*," saith *Pliny*. If I might heere presume to insert my humble Advice, I should assure your *Lordships* that there wants nothing more to the suppressing of these Vipers, so ill affected to the *State*, then the hanging up one of their prick-eard Printers here; and the intreating the *Vnited States*, in his *Maiesties* name, to proclaime some great punishment, both against body & goods, against all such as shall either write, or print, any thing factious against him selfe, his *Church*, or *State*. I beleeve, my *Lordes*, the *States* would not iudge it seemly, nor safe, to deny our *Royall Master* this Request. In my Knowledge, *Amsterdam*

[marginal note:] Pliny.

is the Nurſe of this, and all other ſerpentine Broodes. In this *Citty*, long ſince I mett wth a two-legged *Church*, an *Engliſh*-Weaver, who held y^t God had but one Regenerate Child in the world, and that was him ſelfe; whom a Souldier, then preſent, confuted, with a very good Cudgell, & made this timerous *Church-Militant* flie into a Cocke-Loft. Were they barred printing at *Amſterdam*, wee are ſure that neither *St Omers*, *Lovaine*, nor *Doway*, ſhould have any of their cuſtome. To threaten the Writers onely with loſſe of eares, will never be a meanes to make them abſtaine from libelling. It would bee a greater loſſe in their eſteeme to have their tongues cut, or their teeth beaten out; for they are unparall'd Scoldes, and moſt tall Trencher-men.

They have good reaſon on their bare knees, wth penitent teares from the bottome of their heartes humbly to praiſe God, that their Treſpaſſe (wch was no better than Treaſon) mett wth ſo mercifull a *King* and *Councell*, as would accept of the eare for the head, wch by Lawe was forfeit'd. And this I will adde, that (in my Conſcience) *Junius Brutus* did not more vnwillingly execute his Children, for conſpiring againſt the Liberty of their Countrey, then your *Lordſhips*, & their other *Judges*, pronounced Sentence on thoſe impudent Delinquents, who have a thouſand Stratagems to vndermine and overthrowe the preſent Governm^{nt} of the *Church*, & conſequently the *CommonWealth*.

Of one thing I will warne them that they want no more of the Grace of GOD, till by effect they manifeſt that they love the Peace of GOD; for till then noe man will beleeve that they have any meaſure of it at all. *St. Paul* in all his *Epiſtles*, ſaveing in that to the *Hebrewes*, where in (for ſome reaſons, beſt knowne to him ſelfe, hee writes commends to no man) placeth Grace before Peace; by wch hee gives vs to vnderſtand, that w^{th}out the Grace of GOD, wee can neither have Peace w^{th}in ourſelves, nor wth others. If then they will not have us argue them of want of Grace, let them, by their Works, give vs good proofe that they love Peace. How precious this Peace is, in GOD's Eyes, Hee ſhewes in creating all other Creaturs by couples, but Man ſingle; that out of him alone all the Humane Race might iſſue; & ſome Jnterpretters, on this very place, affirme that Hee myſtically commended vnto vs, hereby, Vnity and Peace. At the Nativity of our SAVIOUR, the Angells declared this Peace to all men; and after His Reſurrection Hee Him Selfe bequeethed it to His Diſciples. Let them therefore pretend Religion no more, vnleſſe they bring Deeds, as well as Wordes, to warrant that they love their neighbour as them

S. Paul.

Gen. i.

S. Matthew.

selves. If they will listen to *St. Iames,* hee will informe them " *that this is true Religion & undefiled before* God, *to visitt the Widdowes and Fatherlesse, &c.*" Envy, that rust of their Soules, will at length consume them; for we all know they fetch this holy Fire, they so much boast of, frō the Divell's Kitchen, who first envying Man for aspiring to that Supreme Place hee fell from, sought to supplant his Happinesse, and to drive him out of the Terrestriall & Celestiall Paradise.

 If for this, my Charitable Advice, they (keeping their owne Custome) return mee ill Language, I must not onely, with Patience, endure it, but applaud my Fate, wch will allowe mee such glorious Companions in my Sufferings, as my *King,* the *Lordes* of His *Councell,* both *Spirituall,* & *Temporall,* and all the *Fathers* of the *Primitive Church.* I will give them good Security never hereafter to reply to any sottish satyricall *Pamphlett* of theirs. They and others complaine that they are not fully answered by Dr *Heylin,* & Mr *Dowe,* and therefore much lesse will they bee satisfied by my vnable penne. The best Tennis-player living cannot shew his cunning, if his Opposer cannot put him to the best of his Play; neiy^{er} can the best Schollar breathing shew his learning in refuting the idle obiections of a shallow Adversary, who denies thinges vniversally granted. The most compendious way of confuting theife Wranglers is to give them the lye. If my Vote might paffe, I would *first* have them anfwered by *Weftminfter* Schollars, *next* by *Eaton*, & fo^e fucceffively, by all the *Free-Schooles* throughout the Land.

I will adde no more, touching my felfe, but this, that I will give the whole body of their *Schifme feaven years* to paralell that *Panegericke* of myne, wch they fo much vilifie, and could wifhe they had another *Robert Wifedome* to helpe them. And I dare them, or any malignant Cenfurer, of what Sect foever, to write *The Bleffed Virgins Story* after mee. I know theife *Simplicians*, out of the iointe Stocke of their witts, are not able to equall it; & therefore turne defpaire into iudgment. Had I debafed her all I could, theife fworne Enemies of all her infinite Graces, had extoll'd mee to the Skies; or had I fuperftitioufly idolatriz'd her, the *Papifts* had both magnified and advanced mee; where as (keeping the middle) I am cryed downe by both the extremes. But I loath all Preferment that muft bee acquired by fwimming againft the Streame of that *Church* from whom I received the *first* Principles of my Religion, w^{ch}, till death, I will preferve entyre. It were a vaine Ambitiõ in mee to feeke to fhunn the common fate of all *Bookes*, " *Laudatur ab his, culpatur ab illis.*"

Femall Glory.

A Just Apology.

To give the world a Testimony that I freely forgive *Burton* and his fellow Martyr, (*Qui bene loqui non didicerunt*) for what they have written, or intended against mee, I have lately dissuaded a Friend of myne from publishing a *Treatise* the Tytle where of is this:—*The Lives of the* three *Crop-Eard* Saints, *who* first *suffered within their Heads,* next *without;* first *lost their Wits,* then *their Eares, &c.*

I most submissively crave yor *Lordships* Pardon, for importuning you wth this weake *Discourse,* vnworthy of your Viewe, and vnable to endure the test of your more profound, and strong Judgments; where in, if I have beene a little too tart, I humbly beseech your *Lordships* to impute it to the extremity of the Wrong done mee.

I will now conclude wth this best of Antidotes against the worst venome Detraction can spit out, " *Regium est male audire, cum benefeceris.*"

Your Lordships

Most humble, loyall Servant,

ANTONY STAFFORD.

𝕱𝖊𝖒𝖆𝖑𝖑 𝕲𝖑𝖔𝖗𝖞:

or,
The Life, and Death of
OUR BLESSED LADY,
The Holy Virgin
𝕸𝖆𝖗𝖞,
GODS *Owne Immaculate* Mother;
To whose Sacred Memory the
Author dedicates these his
humble Endeavours:

A Treatise worthy the reading & meditation of all modest Women, who live under the Government of Vertue, & are obedient to her Lawes.

By ANTH: STAFFORD, Gent.

"𝕬 𝖂𝖔𝖒𝖆𝖓 shall compass a 𝕸𝕬𝕹."—JER. xxxi. 22.

LONDON:
Printed by *Thomas Harper*, for *Iohn Waterson*, and are
to be sold at his Shop in *Pauls* Church-
Yard, at the signe of the
Crowne. 1635.

"O *Mother Maide*, O *Maide* and *Mother* fre,
O *Bushe* unbrent, brenning in *Moyses* sight,
That ravishedst doun fro the DEITEE
Thurgh their humblesse the gost that in thee alight.

. . . . .
. . . . .

Lady, thy bountie, thy magnificence,
Thy vertue, and thy gret humilitie
Ther may may no tong expresse in no science.

. . . . .
. . . . .

My Conning is so weke, O blisful *Queene*,
For to declare thy grete worthinesse
That I ne may the weighte not sustene."
     CHAUCER, *The Prioress' Tale.*

A Table
of the Principall Things
handled in this History.

THE Preface to the *New Edition;* containing *some Account of* The Femall Glory, & *its* Author; *the Attacks upon the Book, by* Henry Burton, & William Prynne; & *the* Defence *thereof, by the Reverends Dr.* Peter Heylin, & *Mr.* Christopher Dow, *B. D.*   P. v

A Just Apology; *or A Vindication of a Booke entituled* The Female Glory, *from the false and malevolent Aspersions cast uppon it by* Henry Burton, *of late deservedly censured in the* Starr Chamber. *By* Anthony Stafford, *Gent.* . . .   Page xix

The Femall Glory; *or the Life and Death of the* Holy Virgin Mary. *By* Anth: Stafford, *Gent.*
Page li

The Epistle Dedicatory, *to the Lady* Theophila Coke . . . .   Page lvij

A TABLE.

To the Feminine Reader . . . . . . Page lxii

To the Masculine Reader . . . . . . ,, lxv

Meditationes, *Poeticæ, & Christianæ, in Annunciatorum* Beatæ Virginis. W. A. . . Page lxx

The Ghyrlond *of the* Blessed Virgin Marie. B. I.
    Page lxxiv

A Pannegyricke *upon the* Blessed Virgin Mary. T. M. . . . . Page lxxvij

Another Panegyricke *on the* Blessed Virgin Mary.
    Page lxxx

A Panegyricke, *dedicated to the Eternall Memory, and glorious Fame of the* Blessed Virgin Mary.
    Page lxxxiii

The Life *of the* Holy Virgin:

Her *externall Beauty* . . . . Page 3
Her *internall Beauty* . . . . ,, 7
Her *Birth* . . . . ,, 11
Her *Infancy* . . . . ,, 17
Her *Betrothing* . . . . ,, 24
The *Salutation* . . . . ,, 26
Her *Prudencie, her opportune Silence, & caution of Speech* . . . . Page 42
Her *Faith* . . . . ,, 47
Her *Obedience* . . . . ,, 51
Her *Humility* . . . . ,, 53
Her *Conception* . . . . ,, 68
Her *Visitation* . . . . ,, 75

A TABLE.

Her Charity . . . . Page 82
Her Delivery . . . . ,, 102
Her Purification . . . . ,, 118
Her Motherly Care, together with her Conjugal Faith & Obedience . . . . . Page 133
Her Demeanour at her SONNE's *Death, & her paſſive Fortitude, & Patience* . . . . Page 135
Her Lamentation . . . . ,, 146
Her Aſſumption . . . . ,, 160

The Authors *Apology for* CHRISTS *Own* Mother
           Page 164
Apoſtrophe Authoris . . . . . . Page 182

"We believe the *Mother* of our LORD to have been not only before and after His Nativity, but also for ever, the most *Immaculate* and *Blessed Virgin*."

BISHOP PEARSON.

"Far be it from any *Christian* to derogate from that special privelege granted her, which is incommunicable to any other. We cannot bear too reverend a regard unto the *Mother* of our LORD, so long as we give her not that worship which is due unto the LORD Himself."

BISHOP PEARSON.

"Making mention of the *All-holy, Undefiled,* and *Most-Blessed Mary, Mother* of GOD, and *Ever-Virgin,* with all Saints, let us commend ourselves, and each other, and our whole life unto CHRIST our GOD."

BISHOP ANDREWS.

The Epistle Dedicatory.

TO THE MOST HAPPY MISTRESSE

of all imaginable Graces, which

beautifie, and ennoble, both

body, and minde, the

LADY THEOPHILA COKE.

Madame,

Y Motives for the Dedication of this enſuing *Treatiſe* to your *Ladiſhip*, are *three*; your Knowledge, your Vertue, and my owne Obligation. For the *firſt*; as it is to you a ſingular Ornament, and Content, ſo is it to me a ſpeciall Comfort; for you cannot delight more to underſtand, then I doe to be underſtood. Had I written to your *Ladiſhip* in the *Roman* Language, the *French*, the *Italian*, or the *Spaniſh*, they had beene almoſt as familiar to you as this your native Tongue, in which you are *Miſtreſſe* of ſo great

The Epistle Dedicatory.

an Elegancy, that no words are so fit as your owne, to eternize your owne Actions. But these are only the conveyances of Learning, the vast body whereof you have fathom'd, and in every severall part of it are *Mistresse* of as much, as the want of an Academicke Education, and the manifold divertments incident to your Sexe, permit. And of this inestimable treasure, Modesty keeps the key, and shuts out Ostentation; not suffering a word to issue forth, without a Grace to attend it. Hence, it comes to passe, that as it is impossible to handle perfumes, without bearing away part of their sent; so, to converse with you, without favouring of your Goodnesse. Nor does your Discourse alone relish of your sweet Disposition; for you reade not of a Vertue, which you forthwith put not into act, and adde to it a greater beauty, then it had in the Example from which you deriv'd it.

The consideration, *Madam*, of these your Excellencies, confirm'd in me a beliefe, that this Portraiture (though imperfect) of the Prime *President* of Femall Perfection, would prove a Present most acceptable to your *Ladiship*, to whose Innocency you make as neer an approach as any thing mortall can doe. Should I say you are without sinne, I should impiously contradict the *Scriptures*. Should I say you have any, I should unjustly goe against mine

The Epistle Dedicatory.

own knowledge; for neither I, nor I think, Envy her felf, could ever yet difcover in you the leaft imperfection. Sure I am, if you have infirmities, they are inteftate, unleffe you place your owne Confcience for a witneffe, which it will not better become to judge it felfe, then it will doe my Charity to cleare it. Nor is this Purity of yours froward, and formall; but gentle, free, and communicative. You fhew the world that there is a Chriftian Freedome, of which we may lawfully partake. By your faire Demeanour you cleerly demonftrate, that Sanctity may be without Aufterity; and Vertue fecurely fociable, and that fhee is more fruitfull in fociety, than in folitude.

This teftimony, *Madame*, Truth, and the people (whofe Regifter I am) commanded mee to give you, and commend to Pofterity. I cannot defcend to fuch bafeneffe, as to flatter you; yet, (if I fhould,) would not you be flatter'd, who are like a fweet Inftrument, that fends forth a delightfull Sound without being fenfible of its owne Harmony. No, no, *Heaven* forbid my lines fhould bee like thofe Sacrifices, out of which they ufed to plucke the heart, but leave the tongue behinde. I ferioufly proteft, that if you were *Empreffe* of the World, and were withall as eminent in Vice, as you are in Vertue, I would not give you the leaft praife in exchange for all your

The Epistle Dedicatory.

large poffeffions; for no gold fhall ever winne mee to guild finne. And I freely confeffe, that if within the large circuit of my Converfation, or Reading, I could have found a feminine Example, fairer then your owne, to her perufall, if living, I had commended this *Treatife*, if dead, had bequeath'd it to her Memory. Such a proftituted Eloquence, as made Apologies for *Meffalina,* and *Quartilla*, are, to me, odious. But wee muft warily diftinguifh betweene a groffe Flattery, and a due Praife; the latter of which, faith *Pliny*, no man contemneth, till hee hath left to doe things praifeworthy. As we cannot over-worfhip the True Deity, fo wee cannot over-praife a true Piety.

It onely now refteth, that I offer up to your *Ladifhip*, *two* Petitions; the *firft* of which is, that you would vouchfafe to permit this *Booke*, under your gratious Patronage, to doe that where you are not, which you performe where you are; that is, to confirme the good, and convert the bad. The *next* is, that your *Ladifhip* would be pleafed to accept of my fubmiffive Gratitude, which, though great, can be no way proportionable to the infinity of your favours. Thefe I would endeavour here to fumme up, were I not deterred from the attempt by Impoffibility, and your nobleft Nature; to which nothing is more difpleafing, than thankes for an old Benefit; nothing more

[margin: Plinius fecundus in Epift.]

pleasing, than the conferring of a new. I choose, therefore, rather to be argued of Ingratitude, than of offending your *Ladishippe*, whose service next to that of GOD, I justly glory in, it being the onely Honour now left,

  Your Ladiships

   Most humble, loyall Servant,

    𝔄𝔫𝔗𝔥. 𝔖𝔱𝔞𝔣𝔣𝔒𝔯𝔡.

To the Feminine Reader.

Y OU are here presented, by an extreme Honourer of your Sexe, with a Mirrour of Femall Perfection. It is not a Glasse, wherein a Babe, a Foole, or a Monster may see it selfe, as well as you. By this, you cannot curle your haires, fill up your wrinckles, and so alter your Looks, that Nature, who made you, knowes you no more, but utterly forgets her owne Workmanship. By this, you cannot lay spots on your faces; but take them out of your Soules, you may. By this, you cannot compose your Countenances; but your Mindes, you shall; and give them a never fading Beauty. In this, you may discerne all Vertues, and all Graces at their full growth. Here, you may discover Charity distributing; Temperancy abstaining; Patience suffering; Humanity yeelding; Chastity resisting; Valour combating; and Prudency assisting all these. Here,

To the Feminine Reader.

any Ornament *you already have, you may better; and any you have not, you may purchase, at the easie rate of reading, and imitating. Here, you may learne to transforme your ugly* Vices, *into as amiable* Vertues.

This Glasse *will not flatter you; nor, if you be angry with it, for shewing your Deformities, can you breake it. Both the matter, and the reflections, here, are all internall; and, therefore, not tangible. This is Shee, whose Embleme, ingenious Antiquity made an* Vnicorne, *laying his head in the lappe of a* Virgin. *This is the faire* Tree; *whose lovely Fruit, once tasted, expels, not for a time onely, but for ever, the Venome of the most deadly sinnes. This is she, who was, on Earth, a* Confirmer *of the good, and a* Reformer *of the reprobate. All her Visitants were but so many Converts, whose bad affections, and erronious opinions, the sweetnesse of her discourse had rectified. The Leprosie of sinne was her daily cure; and they (whom Vice had blinded) were, by her, restored to their inward sight, and their prostrate Soules adored Divine, Majesticall* Vertue, *residing in this Sacred* Temple. *The Conference with her, rais'd them above themselves; and enfranchis'd their Soules, till then, chained to their bodies. The knowledge of her, humbled the most proud natures; for the lustre of her Merits, render'd their owne obscure. O make the emulation of this chaste* Turtle *your onely study! and not in words onely, but in deeds also shew your selves Proficients; for Vertues meditated, and not acted, do but puffe us up the more, wee easily beleeving, that wee are what we resolve to be.* On this, ground your beliefe, that *shee amongst you who shall constantly tread in her paths, shall at length arrive at the Celestiall Paradice which now she inhabits, and shall receive this Salutation, not from an Angell, but from* GOD *Himselfe;* Welcome, thou faire Soule, full of Grace, enter into the Glory, I have prepared for thee.

To the Masculine Reader.

OR to you alſo (though of a different Sexe) this *Booke* belongs, to whom the Sacred *Subject* of it brought the ſame Eternall Benefit, ſhee did to her owne kinde. Neither doth ſhe onely require your Gratitude, but your Imitation, whoſe meaneſt Perfection farre excels all your ſo long vanted maſculine merits. I doubt not, but by the more, and leſſe knowing of you, I ſhall be diverſly judged. The *firſt* will argue mee of Indiſcretion, in that I choſe not a Matter of a higher nature, whereby to make a demonſtration of my ſufficiency. To theſe I ſhape this anſwer, that my Invention could not ſoare higher; for whether wee regard her Perſon, or her divine Gifts, ſhee is, in Dignity, next GOD Himſelfe. There is nothing of ſo ſublime a ſtraine as Vertue, which enters Heaven, when Subtility, and Curioſity are juſtly excluded. It is Vertue muſt

save us; for in knowledge, the Divell himselfe farre exceeds us. There is no Argument, as I take it, so important, or concernes us so much, as that of our Salvation. These men would have mee busie my selfe in the Physicks, to finde out of what—not wherefore I am made: Or in the Mathematickes, to learne how farre it is to Heaven—not how to come thither: Or in Divinity, to bee inquisitive whether, or not CHRISTS miraculous feeding of so many, was by Augmentation, or Multiplication, of the Loaves and Fishes: Whether or no they who were born with sight, & afterwards lost it, being restored to it againe by CHRIST, saw better after the Cure, than they did before their Blindenesse; And whether or no the Dead, who rose with our SAVIOUR, ascended with Him, or were againe reduc't to Dust.

To these needlesse accute follies, I aspire not. How many are there now in Hell, who while they liv'd here, were esteem'd the Organs of the Sciences, the Temples of Wisedome, nay Oracles, as if they had beene form'd in Heaven, and sent downe hither full fraught with GODS Owne Secrets, yet now detest their former vaine Knowledge, as much as the Darkenesse they lived in? But in this kingdome of Woe and Horrour, none of Vertues subiects ever resided. Let them therefore censure on, they shall not so much as shake my security; for I know it fares with univerfall Learning, as with the Vniverfe, wherein there are more Delinquents then Iudges.

The opinions of thefe I can well tollerate, becaufe they proceed from Science, though erronious. But there are fome whom I have heard to paffe their cafting Verdicts on the moft meriting *Authors*, who deferve themfelves to bee hang'd, for fo often violating their owne mother tongue, did not their ignorance pleade their pardon. Let thefe poore wretched things, who, what they heare in the laft company, vent for their owne in the next, fhare amongft them my fcorne, and pitty, as being far below my anger. I am not ignorant that he who feares the pale meager Family of the *Zoili*, muft onely write to his owne *Lar*. If to the truely Vertuous, the truely Underftanding, I can approve thefe my humble Indeavours, and draw any *one* Soule, but *one* degree nearer to Goodneffe, my holy ambition, and my no fmall labour, fhall receive an ample fatisfaction.

It now remaines that as to thefe latter, I feeke to approve all my actions, fo to them I likewife effay to iuftifie this prefent Worke. I am the *firft* (to my knowledge) who hath written in our vulgar tongue on this our *Bleffed Virgin*, drawne thereto I confeffe by the ftrength rather of affection, than of ability.

To the Masculine Reader.

Yet, withall, I professe that I am her Admirer, not her Idolater; and that I no way allow of their profane custome, who robbe GOD of His Honour, and bestow it on her. But this I will say, that though I impute not the late troubles, and afflictions, of the *Protestant Party* in *Germany*, to the small reverence there paid her (many of GODS Iudgements according to *Saint Austin*, being secret, none unjust); yet, truly, I beleeve that the undervaluing of *One* so Great, and Deere in CHRISTS Esteeme, cannot but bee displeasing to Him; and that the more we ascribe to her (setting Invocation apart) the more gratious we appear in His Sight. I have beene as cautious in the penning of this *Treatise*, as possibly I could, and (in imitation of Vertues own selfe) have kept the meane. But all pretenders to Divinity know, that without the helpe of Ecclesiasticall History, we can speake little of her Life, or Death; so sparing is the *Holy Writ*, in the mention of her. The *Scholasticall*, and *Ecclesiastical Writers* inserted in this Booke to trust, or distrust too much, is alike erronious; and therefore I referre all to the discretiõ of the *Reader*.

I will onely adde this, that since the finishing of this *Story*, I have read a *Booke* of the now *Bishop* of *Chichester*, entituled *Apparatus*, &c. and am glad to finde that I have not digressed

S. Austin.

To the Masculine Reader.

from him in any one particular. I conclude with this Proteftation, that if I have fwerved in any, the leaft, point from the Tenents received in the *Englifh Church*, I fhall bee moft ready to acknowledge my felfe a true Penitent. Farewell.

Meditationes,

Poeticæ & Christianæ, in Annunciationem

Beatæ Virginis,

M. A.

Aue Maria.

AVISA es quondam, perque omnia secula gaude,
  Omnia quæ gaudi secula tempus habet.
    Stipasti quæ lætitia castum aluear alui.
Æquum est lætitiæ mella ut in aure bibas.
Tu gaudi Verbum peperisti, & dicit Avete
  Omnibus: atque omnis terra revibrat Ave.
Sed tu salvificum genuisti in secula Salve:
  Nostra eccho nudum nomen bonoris, Ave.

Gratia Plena.

Quam sunt plena suo distenta alvearia melle,
  Quod flore e vario Chymica stillat apis:

In Annunciationem Beatæ Virginis.

Quam plena est adamante suo, teres area gemmæ,
  Quæ quod non recipit, prensat amore decus:
Quam plena est radijs solaribus aurea luna,
  Oppositum toto cum bibit orbe jubar:
Quam plena est Charitum, Charitum modulata chorea,
  Tam plena est decoris Virgo Maria Dei.
Invide quid fontem crispas? mirabile non est
  Si gravida est Charitum, qua gravidata Deo *est.*

Dominus tecum.

Humani lapsum generis sub tristibus umbris
  Luxerat Angelici curia tota chori,
Et reparari iterum coniuncti numinis ansa
  Virgineo optavit posse videre sinu.
O homo quam sit grata salus tibi propria! quando
  Angelica exultat turba salute tua.

Benedicta tu in mulieribus.

Morborum mors intravit longo ordine mundum,
  Fæminea quondam solicitata manu:
Sic Charitum Vita intravit longo agmine mundum,
  Fæminea Mariæ solicitata fide.
Fons nobis vitæ, vitā pariendo fuisti:
  Nosque erimus laudis fons, benedicta tibi.
Nam dignum est per quam cæpit benedictio vitæ,
  Vt sit præ sexu ter benedicta suo.

Et Benedictus Fructus Ventris tui.

Eructasse bonum pleno de pectore Verbum,
  Divino sese prædicat ore Pater.

Hoc Christus *Verbum est, quod de bonitatis abysso,*
 Effudit casto Virgo Maria *sinu.*
Gratum est, & iustum pariter, Benedictio ut ipsa
 Fusa repercusso sit benedicta sono.

Spiritus Sanctus superveniet in te.

Vt Zephiri teneris ubi sibilat halitus hortis,
 Dulcis adoratæ depluit aura rosæ:
Spiritus at flori tam molliter oscula libat
 Vt non Virgineos explicet ore sinus:
Sic Mariam Sanctus Deitatis Spiritus *afflat:*
 Numina & castus flumina fundit onyx.
Nec tamen æterni solvit tibi claustra pudoris:
 Statque tuæ implicito culmine turbo rosæ.
Christum *illibata de Virgine credite natum;*
 Sic illibato est cortice natus odor.

Et Virtus Altissimi obumbrabit tibi
Epigramma dissertum.

Vt genuit magnum Pater extra tempora natum:
 Tempore sic natum Virgo Maria brevem.
Prodijt in mundum sibi par, substantia dispar:
 Vt sine Matre Deus, *sic sine patre Puer.*
Grande puerperium Deus *est: maiusque videtur*
 Non eguisse viro, non eguisse Deâ.
Casta fugit lucem, Virgo paritura sub umbrâ:
 Et paritura umbram prestitit ipse Deus.
O condescensus nova gratia: luminis Author
 Ipse creaturæ vertitur umbra suæ.

In Annunciationem Beatæ Virginis. | lxxiii

Vtque invisibilis lucis Pater author habetur.
  Sic est visibilis Virgo Maria *genus.*
Visurus numen Moses *penetravit in umbram:*
  Tunc Christus *numen tunc Pater umbra fuit.*
Migremus tenebræ ad lucem, dum nomine verso,
  Proque die tenebra est, pro tenebraque dies.

The Ghyrlond of the
BLESSED VIRGIN MARIE.

ERE, are five *letters in this Blessed Name,*
Which, chang'd, a five-fold Mysterie designe,
The M. the Myrtle, A. *the* Almonds *clame,*
R. Rose, I. Ivy, E. *sweet* Eglantine.

These forme thy Ghyrlond. Wherof Myrtle green,
  The gladdest ground to all the numbred-five,
Is so implexed, and laid in, between,
  As Love, here studied to keep Grace alive.

The second string is the sweet Almond *bloome*
  Ymounted high upon Selinis *crest:*
As it, alone, (and onely it) had roome,
  To knit thy Crowne, and glorifie the rest.

The third, *is from the garden call'd the* Rose,
  The Eye of flowers, worthy, for his scent,

The Ghyrlond of the Blessed Virgin.   lxxv

To top the fairest Lillie, now, that growes,
  With wonder on the thorny regiment.

The fourth is humble Ivy, intersert,
  But lowlie laid, as on the earth asleep,
Preserved, in her antique bed of vert,
  No faith's more firme, or flat, then, where't doth
      creep.

But, that which summes all, is the Eglantine,
  Which, of the field is clep'd the sweetest Brier,
Inflam'd with ardor to that mystick Shine,
  In Moses Bush, un-wasted in the Fire.

Thus, Love, and Hope, and burning Charitie,
  (Divinest Graces) are so entermixt,
With od'rous sweets and soft Humilitie,
  As if they ador'd the Head, wheron th'are fixt.

The Reverse
on the other side.

THESE Mysteries do point to three more great,
  On the reverse of this your circling Crowne,
All pouring their full showre of Graces downe,
The Glorious TRINITY in VNION met.

Daughter, and Mother, and the Spouse of GOD,
  Alike of Kin, to that most Blessed TRINE,
  Of PERSONS, yet in VNION (ONE) Divine.
How are thy gifts, and graces blaz'd abroad!

The Ghyrlond of the Blessed Virgin.

Most holy, & pure Virgin, Blessed Mayd,
 Sweet Tree of Life, King Davids Strength and Tower,
 The House of Gold, the Gate of Heavens power,
The Morning-Star whose light our Fal hath stay'd,

Great Queen of Queens, most mild, most meek, most wise,
 Most venerable. Cause of all our joy.
 Whose chearfull look our sadnesse doth destroy,
And art the spotlesse Mirrour to Mans eyes.

The Seat of Sapience, the most lovely Mother,
 And most to be admired of thy Sexe,
 Who mad'st us happy all, in thy reflexe,
By bringing forth God's Onely Son, no other.

Thou Throne of Glory, beauteous as the Moone,
 The rosie Morning, or the rising Sun,
 Who like a Giant hasts his course to run,
Till he hath reach'd his two-fold point of Noone.

How are thy Gifts and Graces blaz'd abro'd,
 Through all the lines of this circumference,
 T'imprint in all purg'd hearts this Virgin sence,
Of being Daughter, Mother, Spouse of God?

         B. J.

A Panegyricke upon the
BLESSED VIRGIN MARY.

WHAT eye dares search the brightnesse of the Sun?
What Pencill draw it? what conception
Is cleane enough, thy Purenesse to descry,
Or strong enough, to speake thy Dignity
Blest *Mother* of our LORD, whose happy state,
None but an *Angel's* tongue did first relate?
Thou wert on earth, a *Starre* most Heavenly bright,
That didst bring forth the SUNNE that lent thee light;
An earthly *Vessell* full of Heavenly Grace,
That broughst forth Life to *Adams* dying race;
For GOD on earth, thou wert a Royall *Throne*;
The *Quarry*, to cut out our Corner Stone;
The chosen *Cloth*, to make his mortall Weed,
Soile blest with Fruit, yet free from mortall Seed.

A Panegyricke upon

In marriage bands thou ledſt a *Virgin* Life;
And though untouch'd, becam'ſt a fruitfull *Wife*.
Though thou to aged *Ioſeph* wert aſſur'd,
No carnall love that ſacred League procur'd,
All vaine delights were farre from your aſſent,
For chaſt by Vow, you ſeal'd your chaſt Intent.
Thus GOD His *Paradiſe* to *Ioſeph* lent,
Wherein to plant the TREE of Life He meant,
To raiſe a Birth miraculous, and by
His Sacred Wayes of Power, diſcloſe that High
And Holy Myſtery, which *Angels* (though
So full of Light) deſir'd to peepe into.
When thou thy MAKER didſt bring forth; and He,
Whoſe Age had beene from all Eternity,
Was borne an INFANT from thy Bleſſed Wombe,
He lay encloſed in that narrow Roome,
Whoſe greatneſſe Heaven & earth could not containe.
Who made the world, and Nature did ordaine,
Was made of thy Fleſh; He, Whoſe open'd Hand
Feeds all the Creatures both by ſea and land,
That even to thee thy life and being lent,
Did from thy Breaſt receive His Nouriſhment.
His Birth no humane tongues were fit to ſing,
Th' Angellike *Quire* did greet their New-Borne KING,

So bright a Confort, and so sweet a Lay
Made night more faire and cheerfull than the day,
And little *Bethlem* with more Glory fill'd,
Than all the *Roman* Pallaces could yeeld.
How wondrous great is then thy happinesse
That wert His *Mother?* but who can expresse
So high a blisse? when we desire to fame
Some other Maid, or vertuous Womans name,
When we of other Ladies write the lives,
Of chaste Maides, happy Mothers, constant Wives,
Such as best Writers have renown'd of yore,
When we have told their noble Vertues o're,
We draw examples, and besides their owne
Faire stories, praise them by comparison.
But in thy life we cannot; thou alone
Canst not at al admit comparison.
So far thy happy Name and Honour lives,
Above all other Mothers, Maids, or Wives,
That 'twere a sinne, when we thy story tell,
So much as once to thinke of Paralell.
Wee'l let thee in thine owne pure Titles live,
And speake no praise of thee, but positive;
As when we say all ages, nations all
Shall thee most Happy among women call,
That of the greatest Blessing GOD ere sent
To sinfull man, thou wert the *Instrument*.

                    T. M.

Another Panegyricke on the

Blessed Virgin Mary.

DOE *not tremble, when I write*
A Mistresse praise; but with delight
Can dive for Pearles into the flood,
Fly through every Garden, Wood,
Stealing the choice of flowrs, & winde,
To dresse her body or her minde;
Nay the Saints *and* Angels *are*
Not safe in Heaven, *till she be faire,*
And rich as they; nor will this doe
Vntill she be my Idoll too:
With this sacriledge I dispence;
No fright is in my Conscience,
My hand starts not, nor do I then
Finde any quakings in my pen,
Whose every drop of inke within,
Dwels as in me, my Parents sinne,

Another Panegyricke, &c.

And prayses on the paper wrot,
Have but conspir'd to make a blot,
Why should such fears invade me now,
That writes on her? to whom doe bow
The Soules of all the Iust, whose place
Is next to GODS, *and in His Face*
All creatures and delights doth see
As Darling *of the* TRINITIE;
To whom the Hierarchy *doth throng,*
And for whom Heaven *is all one song.*
Ioyes should possesse my Spirit here,
But pious ioyes are mixt with feare.
Put off thy shooe, 'tis Holy Ground,
For here the flaming Bush *is found,*
The misticke Rose, *the Iv'ry* Tower,
The morning Star, *&* David's Bower,
The Rod *of* Moses, *and of* Iesse,
The Fountaine *sealed,* Gideons Fleece,
A Woman *cloathed with the* Sunne,
The beauteous Throne *of* Solomon,
The Garden *shut, the living* Spring,
The Tabernacle *of the* King,
The Altar *breathing sacred Fume,*
The Heaven *distilling Honie-combe,*
The untouch'd Lilly, *full of Dew,*
A Mother, *yet a* Virgin *true,*
Before, and after she brought forth
(Our RANSOME *of Eternall Worth)*
Both GOD *&* Man, *what Voice can sing*
This Mystery, or Cherubs wing

Another Panegyricke, &c.

Lend from his golden Stocke, a Pen
To write, how Heaven *came downe to men?*
Here feare, and wonder so advance
My Soule, it must obey a Trance.

A Panegyricke,

dedicated to the eternall Memory,
and glorious Fame of the
BLESSED VIRGIN MARY.

END me *Elias* Chariot to inspire
My feeble Muse. Wheeles of Celestiall Fire
Beare her from Earth, purge ev'ry looser thought
This duller ayre, or that grosse dunghill wrought.
Let all her straines be pure, cloath her in white,
And innocent wit; let her chaste Soule delight
In no adulterate line, no wanton sense,
Let all her knowledge be her Innocence,
As *Adams* ere he fell; then will she raise
A Maiden Spirit, to chant a *Virgins* Praise.
Yet let her not be barren, but bring forth
Zeale, to each eare she strikes, so shall her worth
Shine like the *Saint* she sings of, wonders doe,
And be as she a *Maide*, and *Mother* too.

A *Panegyricke*, dedicated to the

Inſtruct me you *nine* Orders how to ſing,
Or let a *Cherubin* pluck me from his wing,
A quill to write the Story, or entreate
Your Brother *Gabriel* from his bleſſed Seate
To viſit Earth, and teach mee, leſt I miſſe
To ſalute *Mary* in a voyce like his.

Sleepe on your eyes, faire Virgins, long hath ſtaid,
Riſe, and to *Bethlem* run, to ſee a *Maide*.
Riſe Matrons, in your armes your Infants beare,
To *Bethlem* haſte, and ſee GODS *Mother* there.
Matrons, and Virgins runne, haſte all to ſee,
Both joyn'd in one, a fruitfull Chaſtity.
Then every Matron this great Wonder tell,
And every Virgin chant a Canticle,
Sing *Bleſſed Marys* praiſe, ſing that for her
IEHOVAH rivall'd with a Carpenter.
Mary, deriv'd from *two* moſt glorious Springs,
The bloud of *Levies Prieſts*, and *Iudahs Kings*,
Which did as in a Type foreſhew her ſtory,*
To be the *Mother* both of Grace and Glory.
Sing of her birth, how not redeem'd with prize,
Her Father payd her as a Sacrifice
Due to his GOD, when others ranſom'd be
With Shekles, as it were a ſlavery
To ſerve their MAKER, and the Parents feare
To truſt Him with the wardſhippe of their Heire.
But the bleſt *Maide* whom *Angels* now admire,

* S. Auſtin, Baronius, *and others, hold that ſhe was deſcended from the Tribe of* Levi, *which the now Biſhop of* Chicheſter *oppoſeth.*

(Glad they have got her to encreafe their Quire)
In child-hood *firft* her *Virgin* tafke begun,
And in the *Temple* pray'd a pretty *Nun*;
That the *firft* breath fhe fuckt was holy aire,
And the *firft* word fhe learn'd to lifpe, was
    Pray'r.
There might you fee an *Infant Saint* out-vie
The *Levites* in Devotion, and an eye
Caft up to *Heaven*, ere it the earth had knowne;
Whole fhowers of teares in pious forrow fhowne
For *Eves* offence, not hers, fhee did begin
To learne Repentance, ere fhee knew to finne.
Each morning ftrove the early Larke, and fhe
Who *firft* fhould chant their Sacred Melody.
He that had feene her might by very fence
Have prophecied an Age of Innocence
Reborne with her. I fhould have thought her
    one
Of the great *Cherubins* fent from its Throne
To breed a race of *Angels*, and fupply
Their roome that fell by proud Apoftafie.
Thus fhe grew up in Zeale, and holy Feares,
Yet ftill Devotion would out-bid her *yeares*,
Till* at *fifteen* (when others holier fires
Grow to more wanton, and unchafte defires)
The *Priefts* bethought a Hufband for her bed;
But *Marys* thoughts all unto *Heaven* were fled.
Yet was fhe *Iofephs Spoufe*, not with th'intent
T'unloofe her Virgin Zone, but to prevent
The futes of others, and enjoy more free

* *The opinion of Mantuan, how true I know not.*

lxxxvi   *A Panegyricke, dedicated to the*

> The treasure of unspotted Chastity.
> Who will beleeve the Wonder I have said?
> *Mary* a Husband tooke, to live a *Maide*.
> Dare not thou *Ioseph* to approach too neare
> This Heavenly *Arke*; thy GOD inhabits there.
> Touch not that sanctifi'd, and hallow'd Wombe,
> Whence thy SALVATION, and the worlds must
>   come:
> For 'tis not, Carpenter, thy Art that can
> Repaire the Fabricke of selfe-ruin'd man:
> *Mary* must *Bride* to thy CREATOUR be,
> And clad in Flesh part of the TRINITY.
> See GOD hath sent from his eternall Sphere,
> Blest *Gabriel*, his fire-wing'd *Messenger*,
> Who crown'd with Glory, and a wreath of
>   Light,
> Salutes the *Virgin*, doubtfull of the sight,

S. Gabriel.   And courts her thus. " *Haile*, Mary, *Full of*
>   *Grace*,"
> (Wherewith a blush rose in her bashfull face,
> And verifi'd his words) " *the* LORD," quoth he,
> " *Hath left His* Heaven, *and comes to dwell in*
>   *thee*;
> " *Blest amongst Women*, *in thy Sexe Divine*;
> " *For ev'ry brest Salvation sucks from thine.*"
> Suppose a *King* had some gay Favorite sent
> With powerfull Rhetoricke, and Court Com-
>   plement
> To win a country girle. What could she guesse
> But 'twas some scorne on her unworthinesse?

Memory of the Blessed Virgin Mary.

So *Mary*, ignorant what her Vertue was,
(For she had made Humility her glasse)
Doubts what the words should meane; wonders to heare
This Salutation; and mistrusts her eare.
And when the *Angell* tels her of a Sonne,
To sit on *Princely Davids* Royall Throne,
To rule the House of *Iacob*, and to be
A sceptred *Prince*, to all Eternity,
Her modest Soule no vaine Ambition sway'd,
She rather chose to live an humble *Maid*,
Then a *Queene Mother.* " *How can I,*" quoth she,   S. Mary.
" *Who nere knew man, and am a* Votary
" *Nere to know any, teeme with such a Birth,*
" *Who would not for the treasure of the earth*
" *Be false unto my Vowes? My Love is Pray'r,*
" *And Piety all the sonnes I meane to beare.*"
But when the *Angell* did Gods Will relate,
That He would get a Sonne that might create,
She yeelds a *Handmaid* to her Lords Desire.
O I but thinke how such strange newes would fire
Some Ladies hearts with pride, when they should heare
Gods growne enamour'd on their beauties were!
How they would thinke themselves worthy the bed
Of their Creatour, and advance their head
Above Mortality, promising their eyes
To be made *Stars* to glorifie the *Skies!*

A Panegyricke, dedicated to the

But *Marys* Zeale swell'd higher then her pride;
Nothing mov'd that, not when old *Zacharys* Bride
Felt the Babe dance, and leape within her wombe,
For joy the *Mother* of his LORD was come,
But bless'd her GOD regarded her estate,
And sung not to her selfe, *Magnificat*.
Nor when the *Shepheards* did relate their story
That was as full of wonder as of Glory,
But tooke the *Angels* Hymne, and chanted then
Glory to GOD on High, good will to men.
Nor when *three Kings* did to her Cratch resort,
Did shee conceive her Stable turn'd a Court,
When to a PRIEST, a PROPHET, and a KING,
They sev'rall brought their sev'rall Offring.
She tooke not to delight a wanton sense.
The pretious Myrrhe, and odrous Frankincense,
Nor did with covetous greedy eyes behold
The Easterne Wealth (the *third* Mans treasure) Gold;
Her SONNE, and SAVIOURS Honour to prefer,
Was Mirrhe, was Frankincense, was Gold to her.
Her life was all Humility; Muse make haste
To sing her Death, and how her life being past,
Heaven entertain'd her; for their Hymnes Divine
Are fitter to relate her praise, than thine.
Thou hast not power t'unfold with what a feare

Memory of the Blessed Virgin Mary. lxxxix

She fled to *Ægypt*, and continu'd there
To save her INFANTS Life, not skill to tell
How much she joy'd at ev'ry Miracle.
Presume not thou to number what her eyes
Showre forth in teares, as on the Crosse she
    spies
Her SONNE, and SAVIOUR, nor what care she
    show'd,
To gather up the drops of Bloud that flow'd
Pure Balsome from His Side; nor venture on
To write with what a violent Zeale she run
To begge with *Ioseph* He a Tombe might have,
By Whom we all are ransom'd from the Grave.
Me thinks I see how by His Crosse she stood,
How her sad eyes vide teares, as He dropt
    Bloud;
Her eyes more sad, cause they retain'd their sight,
And could not doe as *Heaven* did, loose their
    light.
Her armes expresse the Crosse whereon He dide,
As if she too meant to be crucifide.
I see her Vaile rent; for it could not be
The Temple should expresse more griefe than
    she.
Me thinkes I heare her plaints.   " O CHRIST   S. Mary.
    that I
" *Should give Thee Flesh; for else Thou could'st*
    not dye!
" *Divinity is from all passion free,*
" *That Thou canst suffer torments, was from mee.*

"*Wherefore Thy* Virgin Mother *here vowes all*
"*Her houres to Prayers, till Thy laſt Trumpet call.*"

And here I crave no pardon, if my penne
Stabbe thoſe preſumptuous, and o're curious men,
Whoſe bold Diſputes dare into queſtion call
What ſonnes ſhe had, and whether Christ was all.
As if a Mortall durſt to *Mary* come,
And court Gods *Widdow*, to prophane her Wombe;
As if the *Mother-Maide* that ſtil gave ore
To be a *Mother*, but a *Maide* no more;
Or ſhe that God and Man had borne, would be
A *Mother* now to beare Humanity;
As ſhe from *Heaven* to earth, her thoughts had caſt,
And could love *Ioſeph*, that had God embrac'd.
No, having layne, great Heavens, Immortall King,
Vnder the Shadow of Thy gratious Wing:
She *Turtle*-like would a chaſte *Widdow* be,
And vow'd to love no other Dove but Thee;
But ever mourn'd Thy abſence, till her eyes
Had ſpent her Soule in teares, and love-ſtrain'd cries,
Crackt her poore heart-ſtrings. Having caſt away

Memory of the Blessed Virgin Mary.

The toylesome burthen of unweldy clay,
With pure, and ayrie pinions, hence she flies,
And forsakes earth, to seeke Thee in the Skyes.
When she arriv'd where her Blest MATE doth dwell:
What *Poets*, *Priests*, or *Prophets* rage can tell
The entertainements, welcomes, joyes have beene,
Vnlesse in *Pathmos* he had Visions seene.
We may suppose that *Angels* clapt their Wings;
Powers and *Dominions* showted; all the strings
Of *Seraphins* tun'd high, lowd Hymnes did play.
A troope of *Virgins* on the *Milky Way*
Met her in snow-white robes, and Convoy had
Legions of *Martyrs*, all in scarlet clad.
Iosuah with *Captaines*, *David* Sainted *Kings*,
All tendred their respects. The Pallace rings
With acclamations, *Eve* runnes forth to see
Whence sprung the FRUIT, cur'd the forbidden Tree.
Sarah makes haste, her *Ladies* Wombe to blesse,
Without whose Birth, the curse of barrennesse
Had laine upon her, though shee had a sonne,
And had brought *twenty Isaacks* forth for *one*.
Rebecca, with the better of her twins,
And *Rachel*, with her *Ioseph* too, begins
To chant her praise. The brave *Bethulian* Dame,
Victorious *Iudith*, to her welcome came
With troopes of *Amazons*. The *Sheban Queene*,

A Panegyricke, dedicated to the

(Who now the new *Ierusalem* had seene)
Runs to the sight, and wistly gazeth on
The *Mother* of the mightier *Solomon*.
There met with *Saints*, and *Angels*, all desire
To bid her welcome, thus, in a full Quire:

Song of the Blessed Ones.

"*Come* Blessed Virgin, *fixe thine eyes upon*
　　"*This glorious Throne*,
"*And on the Right Hand, there behold thy* SONNE.

"*Behold His Hands, His Feet, His pierced Side*,
　　"*That for us dide*,
"*Whose very Wounds in* Heaven *are* Deifide.

"*Those glorious Lips, which once drew Milke
　　from thee*,
　　"*Shall one day be*
"*The Doome of Soules, to Blisse, or misery.*

"*Blest Wombe, the Mysteries that sprung from
　　hence*,
　　"*Dazle our sense*,
"*Whose onely Essence is Intelligence.*

"*Finite thou wert, yet Infinite in thee*
　　"*Wee treasur'd see*,
"*Mortall, yet* Mother *to Eternity.*

"*Thy* SONNE *made of thee, made thee.* Faith
　　aspire
　　"*One ladder higher*,
"*Elder then's* Mother, *Antient as His* SIRE.

Memory of the Blessed Virgin Mary.

" 'Tis ſtrange thou ſhould'ſt both Maide and
                Mother be;
        " Stranger to ſee
" In one Soule both GOD, and Humanity.

" As Hee was GOD, thou ſtill art Mayd. Who can
        " This Wonder ſcan?
" Hee made thee Mother, as Hee was but Man.

" Thou ſucckl'ſt Him upon thy breaſts, and He
        " To ranſome thee,
" Open'd His Side upon His Paſſion Tree.

" Come Bleſſed Virgin, and receive thy Crowne
        " Of full Renowne,
" Where Death, and Time have laid their
        Scepters downe.

" There ſing with us, how THREE doe ſit upon
        " The glorious Throne;
" ONE of which THREE is TWO, yet ALL but
    ONE."

THUS, Holy *Virgin*, have I ſhadow'd o're
    Thy Picture, in a rude unpolliſht ſcore,
That wiſh'd t'have limm'd it with as lively grace,
As ever Painter drew the ſweeteſt face.
Yet would I not idolatrize thy Worth,
Like ſome, whoſe ſuperſtition ſets thee forth
In coſtly ornaments, in cloaths ſo gay,
So rich as never in the Stable lay.

These make thy Statues now as famous be
For pride, as thou wert for Humility.
I cannot thinke thy *Virgin* Bashfulnesse
Would weare the *Lady* of *Lorettos* dresse,
Though farre more glorious robes to thee were given,
Meekenesse, and Zeale on Earth, Glory in *Heauen.*

Take then the Honour thou hast justly wonne,
Praise above *Angels*, but below thy SONNE.

The Life of
The Blessed Virgin Mary.

Virgine Madre, Figlia del tuo FIGLIO!
Umile ed alta più che creatura,
Termine fiſſo d'eterno conſiglio;
　Tu ſe' colei che l'umana natura
Nobilitaſti sì, che'l ſuo Fattore
Non diſdegnò di farſi ſuà fattura;
　Nel Ventre tuo ſi raccefe l'amore
Per lo cui caldo nell' eterna pace
Coſi è germinato queſto fiore;
　Qui ſe' a noi meridiana face
Di caritade, guiſo intra mortali
　Se' di ſperanza fontana vivace.

Dante.

The Femall Glory:
OR,
The life of the Bleſſed Virgin MARY.

HER EXTERNALL BEAUTY.

ISTORY offers to our view, Myriads of Holy Virgins in Beauty, and Vertue equally attractive, whoſe due Praiſe the *Catholike Church* doth at this day ſolemnely ſing, but with a more elevated Voyce (as Duty on our part, and Merit on hers commands) the Laud of that moſt excellent *Princeſſe*, the *Virgin Mother* of GOD. There be who affirme, that what ever the CREATOR ſaw beautifull in Heaven, or earth, He beſtowed in the

limming of this rare *Piece*; not that she might be stiled the most faire amongst the daughters of women, but by a Heavenly prerogative, the alone Faire, the alone Lovely. Looke how many parts, so many arts you might discerne, of the Celestiall Limmer. And this is no way repugnant to Reason it selfe; for if CHRIST was faire above the Sonnes of men, should not she be so above their Daughters, since from her alone He received His Flesh? *Gregory Nazianzen* proclaimes that she surpass'd all women in lovelinesse. *Andræas* sayes that she was a *Statue* carved by GOD's Own Hand. Others, of those first, and purer times, not without Admiration, observe that GOD was almost fifty Ages in the Meditation of the structure of this stately *Pallace*. And truely our beliefe may easily digest this, that His Omnipotency would make her fit to be the *Mother* of His SON; *Empresse* of this lower world; and the Blessed *Conduit*, through which should passe the Mystery of mans Redemption. Yet finde I a ridiculous description of her in *Epiphanius* a

Galatinus.

S. Gregory Nazianzen.

Andræas.

S. Epiphanius.

Prieſt of *Conſtantinople*; who affirmes, that her face was of the colour of Wheate; her viſage, long; and her noſe, ſutable; her haire, yellow; and her eye-browes, blacke. But what Authority he hath for this, neither I, nor I thinke he himſelfe can well tell; for ſurely ſimple Antiquity was not either curious, or ſkilfull to deliver it by Tradition, or picture, to poſterity. I verily beleeve he had it from his owne dreames, or rather fancy. *Mopſa* is as much beholding to our incomparable, and inimitable *Sydney* for a delineation, as is my Divine *Subject* to this curious Impertinent. Whether her Beauty chiefly conſiſted in colour, in Symmetry of parts, or both, I know not: ſure I am the Streame of other more judicious, pious *Authors* carries me not into an opinion, but a ſtrong beleefe of her Heavenly Forme. *Cardinall Cajetan*, and *Galatinus*, (with what truth I cannot ſay) certainely with more probability then he, maintaine that her excellent Temperature, her conformity of Members, her firme and conſtant Complexion, free'd her from

<small>Cardinal Cajetan & Galatinus.</small>

Dyonifius. all contagion and difeafes. And *Dyonifius* goes further, affirming that fhe was no other then a walking *Spring*. Such variety of fweet Odours her very pores breath'd out on all that came neare her; as we reade of *Alexanders* living body, and the *Ægyptian* Carkaffes, which by a thin fpare dyet obferved in life, even after death fent forth a moft fweet Perfume. *Sylvanus Razzius*

Sylvanus Razzius. recounts a pleafing ftory of a certaine *Clerke*, who by many Prayers implor'd, and obtain'd the Bleffing of her fight; but with this Condition, that he fhould fee her but with one eye, and that one he fhould lofe. He willingly embrac't it; but when fhe appear'd dreft in all her Beames, not being able with one eye to take a full view of her, he opened the other alfo; chufing rather to forfeit his fight for ever, then to loofe one minute of the inconceiveable content he enjoyed in the fight of fo glorious a Spectacle. Were this true, it would make a brave example of a devout Soule, ravifht with the view of a Divine *Object*.

HER INTERNALL BEAUTY.

F the *Inne* was so splendent, so sumptuous, what may we thinke of the amiable *Guest*, that lodg'd in it; her Minde, beset with thoughts cleare, and radiant as her owne eyes? He that dares attempt the expression of these her internall Gifts, is ignorant of her Sublimity; he who dares not, knows not her humanity, her sweetnesse. As no stile can ascend so high as her exalted Worth; so on the other side, none can descend so low as her Humility. Encourag'd therfore by her Meeknesse, not my owne sufficiencie, I shall endeavour to limme her Soule in little (since, in great, neither my time, nor ability will let me), which will appeare an enterprise as hardy,

and vaine as his who fhould ftrive to limmit the Light, or circumfcribe the Ayre. Know then, modeft *Reader* (and receive this knowledge with the fame Extafie, and Zeale I write it) that her internall Lufter was farre greater then her externall; like in this unto the Tents of *Kedar*, as foone cover'd with duft, and almoft burned up with the heat of the Sunne, as foone beaten, and fhaken with tempeftuous weather; but, in the meane time, inwardly all glittering with Glory, and Magnificence. O ye *Angels*, to you it is onely given, not to finne; but on her is conferr'd what you cannot merit, to beare the Reparation of mans ruine. The *Apoftles*, thofe holy *Tapours* of the *Primitive Church*, fometimes burnt dimme, and were obfcur'd with the fogge of finne; but her Brightneffe nothing vitious could leffen, much leffe utterly extinguifh. She was, indeed, Vertues prime, and great Example; and all the accomplifht women of the Ages paft, prefent, or to come, have grace, and happineffe to the full, in being called her imperfect Coppies.

Her Internall Beauty.

 Here my Invention treads a Maze, and my heart is divided betweene an earnest desire to praise her to the height, and a holy feare, lest in that praise, I should trench, on GODS Own peculiar Attributes. That she was no way inferiour to her SONNE, according to the Flesh, I dare not, with some, avouch, who magnifie her in a phrase that violates her Modesty, and makes her blush at her owne Exaltation. Her Lowlinesse was such, that it was nearer the rejecting of all commendations, then entertaining a comparison betweene her selfe, and Him to Whom she had professed her selfe an *Hand-maid*. And no lesse is her shame, or rather, indeed, her trembling, when pennes, prophanely prodigall, ascribe that honour to her which is onely proper, and due to that DEITY from Which she received her Grace, and being. I will not, with *Lipsius* ascribe as much to her Milke, as to her SONNES Bloud. Neither dare I side with those who averre, that she is halfe of that Sacrifice that ransom'd us, and GODS Partner here. Nor is my penne so impiously valiant, as to jus-

<small>Lipsius.</small>

tifie that God made Himselfe the Patterne, and communicated to her by Grace, whatsoever Hee had by Nature. Nor am I of his bold opinion who sayes: If man had never sinned, yet Christ should have taken Flesh, to honour her. These men would have her, in all things, equall to Christ Himselfe. Neither her Modesty, nor mine will admit of this blasphemous flatterie. I willingly allow her to be the *Vessell*, but not the *Fountaine* of Grace. I am much taken with his tenent who holds that God made all things for the use of Man; because He would amply furnish him with matter enough to busie his head, lest he should bee so audacious as to enquire into His Secrets, & encroach upon His Prerogatives. We need not (thanks to His infinite Goodnesse) bee so dangerously venturous, since He affords us a large scope, and ground enough safely to extol this His *Favourite*, second to none that ever bore flesh, either in her owne Desert, or His Esteeme.

HER BIRTH.

O begin with her Birth; it was miraculous, as it alwayes falls out where Nature failes, and GOD fupplies, as He did here in *Anna* the bleffed mother of this more Bleffed *Maid*. And here, by the way, I muſt inſert an obſervation derived from GODS Sacred Word, that for the moſt part the children of ſterility are fruitfull in Sanctity, and all good works. *Samſon* was the ſonne of barrenneſſe; and kept the people in obedience. So was *Iſaac*; and gave precepts to the ſeed of *Abraham*. So was *Samuel*; and foretold the miſery of ſervitude to the *Iewiſh* Synagogue. So was *Ioſeph*; and with his counſell, govern'd all *Ægypt*. So was our Hallow'd *Subject*, who brought forth the

That Ioacimus *and* Anna *were her parents, is an undoubted Truth, received by the* Church, *as wee find both in* Baronius *and* Biſhop Montacute, *in his Booke called* Apparatus, &c.

Sonne of Glory. The flaves of the *Tyrians* rebelling againft their Mafters, and having fubdu'd them, by a generall confent decreed, that hee amongft them who, the next morning, could firft difcover the Sunne rifing, fhould be their *King*. One of them of a more gentle difpofition then the reft, having hidden his Mafter (by name *Strato*) from the others fury, fecretly afkt his advife in this fo important affaire, who bade him look into the *Weft* for there he fhould fooner difcern the approach of the Sunne, then they who fought him in the *Eaft*. This wife counfell he obey'd; and while the reft fixed all their eyes on the *Eaft*, he from the higheft part of the *City*, by his Rayes in the *Weft*, firft difcover'd his afcenfion in the *Eaft*. So in *Anna* (the happy mother of this *Wonder* of women) being then in the occident, or fet of life, the Prophetick world forefaw the brightneffe of the dazeling *Light* fhe then teem'd with. At length the worlds greedy expectation was fatisfied; and this *Cynthia*, this chaft Starre was delivered of a *Plannet* farre greater, and brighter

Her Birth.

then her selfe; of whose all gladding Shine, the first man participated, and the last shal. I may as properly as dolefully call them *Plannets*, since they never rested; but were in perpetuall motion while, in this lower Orbe, they ran their fatall courses, in which they were often clowded, never quite eclipsed.

The day of the Nativity of this most perfect of *Saints*, I finde thus described by *Nicolaus Vernulæus* a late Writer, and a professor of Eloquence. The description I onely insert for the elegancy; for I must condemn it as guilty of levity and vanity, and no way sutable to the Majesty, Gravity, and Modesty of this our Sacred *Subject*.

" *The* Sunne *(saith he) this day burnisht* Nicolaus Vernulæus.
" *his face, the better to illustrate the world,*
" *and to appeare gracious in her sight, who*
" *carried in her breast a Fire purer, and*
" *clearer, than his owne Rayes. The* Earth
" *put on her freshest greene; and the* Flowers
" *spread their dainty leaves, and made a*
" *sweet exchange of odours with her; yet*
" *hung their heads to see themselves both*
" *in colour, and sent, so farre surpass'd.*

" The Trees *advanc'd their curled heads,*
" *and compos'd their lookes within the*
" *chriſtall ſtreames, who seemed to dance*
" *after their owne mumur. Amongſt the*
" Beaſts, *their* King *layd by his fierceneſſe;*
" *and not one of his ſubiects was found*
" *ſavage, or polluted that day. Then was*
" *the* Proverbe *croſs'd; for the* Worme *be-*
" *ing trod on, would not turne againe, leſt ſhe*
" *ſhould prove unlike her meekeſt* Miſtreſſe.
" *In the very bowels of the* Earth, *the* Mine-
" rals *and the* Stones *more pretious, aſſumed*
" *their quicker ſparkes, as Emblems of her*
" *ſplendour. The* Ocean *had not a wrinckle*
" *in his face; thouſands of* Halcions *ho-*
" *ver'd o're his head; and his* Tritons
" *blew ſo lowd, that their notes ſounded the*
" *very bottome of the Deep. Within his*
" *vaſt* Dominions *was no diſcord that*
" *day; for the greater of the* Fiſh *forſooke*
" *their prey, and the ſmaller ſwumme in*
" *that ſecurity, that the* Sprat *bearded the*
" Dolphin, *and playd with the noſe of the*
" *overgrown* Whale. *The* Birds *ſung their*
" *choiſeſt aires; the* Fowles *flew nearer the*
" *earth to ſalute her; and their towring*

Her Birth.

"Lord, *the* Eagle, *brought his young ones*
"*to try their eyes at this new borne* Light.
"*The* Ayre *it selfe was like her, gentle;*
"*and being invisible, came to steale a kisse*
"*from her cherry lips, soft and smooth as*
"*were his owne. The* Windes (*conceiving*
"*their silence would best please*) *kept them-*
"*selves within their dens; onely* Zephirus
"*was let loose to fanne the* Pinke, *and* Violet,
"*and play the wanton with the* Rose."

Thus farre *Vernulæus*. Of all things created, man alone, to whom, being sicke, she was to bring a Soveraine ANTIDOTE was found least joyfull, least gratefull. Yet were there some, no doubt, of Gratitudes children, who lay prostrate before her; and did homage to their sweetest *Lady*, who might better be called the *Mother* of the living, then *Eve*; since she, like a Murdresse, gave her children death ere birth; and defaced those Images whereon GOD had set His Owne Stampe. She was no wiser than a poor *Fly*, who, enamour'd of the beanty of the flame, longs to try if it be as sweet as faire, and is consumed with her owne folly. Had our Blessed *One* supplied her roome in *Paradice*, the forbidden Fruit had, perchance, beene yet untasted, and man uncursed; for she was altogether void of Curiosity, proper to that weaker sexe, and the very bane of it. Our dearest *Princesse* therefore, was deservedly a *Queene* ere borne; receiv'd a Crowne sooner than sight; and found her Throne seated upon the threshold of life. And what Crowne was she presented with? Not one, to compose which, the *East*, and the *West* joyned their treasures; but a Crowne in the making whereof every Vertue, and all the Graces had a hand. Nor did any vaine mortall place it on her Sacred Temples, but God Himselfe; Who thought nothing too deare, nor omitted any ornament that might embellish this goodly *Edifice*, wherein Himselfe meant to reside. Having thus adorn'd, and honour'd her, He plac'd her in this lower world, for the good and admiration of all, for the conversation of a few. Though borne on earth she lived here like a Native of *Heaven*.

HER INFANCY.

S we may gueſſe at the neatneſſe of a houſe, by the entry into it: ſo we may judge of her lifes remainder, by the very beginning. *Sabellicus* affirmes that ſhe no ſooner ſaw the light, but ſhe ador'd the CREATOR of it; and lifted up her heart and eyes, to the great INFUSER of all her incomparable Excellencies. She lov'd GOD, ere ſhe had ſeene man. The defect of her tongue could not hinder the operation of her Soule; in which, ere ſhe could ſpeake, ſhe acknowledg'd His unſpeakeable Goodneſſe. In her, *Religion* preceded the uſe of reaſon; and ſhe apprehended GOD's Mercies, long ere ſhe was capable of His Nature, and Wiſedome.

Sabellicus ſets downe how ſhee diſpos'd of every particular hour.

Ere ſhe could utter holy Words, ſhe made holy Signs, by which ſhe made knowne the ſanctity of her Heart. The firſt word ſhe learn'd to liſpe, was IEHOVAH. She ſent forth many a ſigh for ſinne, not having committed any; and bewailed that, of which ſhe was utterly ignorant. The rowling of the Cradle, put her in minde, that ſhe was newly enter'd into the tempeſt of this life; the infinite dangers whereof to eſcape, ſhe made Vertue her Pilot.

We will not here with ſome Writers of her Life, diſpute whether or no, ſhe had the ſame ordinary Education with other children; nor, with them affirme, that ſhe entred the *Temple* at three yeares old, and lived cloſe by the *Altar*, and was fed Miraculouſly by an *Angell*; as alſo that it was there revealed to her, that ſhe ſhould be deliver'd of the MESSIAS. I will not make one ſteppe out of GOD's Own Path, frō which I never yet ſaw the greateſt wit to ſwerve, but it was in danger of ſticking faſt. Yet hath a pious Charity often ſwallowed more than all this. If from the

Her Infancy.

hand of an *Angell* she there received food naturall, or supernaturall; sure I am the Wonder is not so great as that of the INCARNATION, where the Wombe included the WORD. And why should we with difficulty beleeve, that this white spotlesse *Soule* was illuminated with Revelations, by the Divine Object of her chaste Vowes? who undoubtedly deserved to be rapt up if it were possible, a story higher than was *Saint Paul*. It is likely enough, saith *Mantuan*, GOD would have the *Temple* of His SPIRIT to dwell in the *Temple* of His Service. The same *Author* affirmes, that she there liv'd a pretty *Nun*; and spunne, and wove the sacred Vestments, till her *eleventh* or *twelfth yeare*; when her Prudency, and Shame, and the care of her Reputation, forbade her to accompany even the very *Priests* themselves, men whom GOD had selected out of the masse of the vulgar to teach His Will, to instruct His people, and to sing His praise. These curiosities, and bold conjectures, let us rather beleeve, then contest with the broachers; for it is Wisedome to grant

[margin: Mantuan.]
[margin: Mantuan.]

what we cannot confute. Let us then imagine, that this holy *Recluse* confined her body to this sacred solitude, and a spare diet; and warily kept her Soule from the surfets to which carnall delights invite all things humane. And it is consonant both to reason and truth, that her Exercise there, was pious like the place. They who goe about to take away her writing, and reading tongue, are impiously ridiculous; since it evidently appeares that she was well read in the *Scriptures*, by her Divine Hymne uttered in *Zacharies* house. On her, Reading attended Meditation; on her Meditation, Prayer; on her Prayer, Action, as the louely Fruit of the precedent. Thus busied, the day left her, the night found her. Her sleeping Cogitations, we may suppose, were sutable to her waking; and her very dreames, Divine. She had not a thought that was her owne; all belong'd to God. She was slow to speake, saith *Sabellicus*; but ready to obey all holy Advice. Her tongue was not so swift as her Wit, which made it follow for direction, in all the requisites of speech.

Ancient and eminent Authors affirme her to have beene learned in the Hebrew tongue, all which you shall finde quoted in Cedrenus.

Sabellicus.

In a word, she might well usurpe that of the *Church*; *When I was a little one, I was pleasing to the* Most High.

When, upon mature deliberation, she left the *Temple*, she still liv'd as if she had beene in it. Though in body she was sociable, she fetter'd her Soule from wandring abroad; her true conversation being in *Heaven*. This flourishing *Vine* planted her selfe amongst the Olives. She was more choice of her Company, then of her food, or rayment; both which, God knows, were course enough. She knew Temperancy to be Gods, and Natures Favorite; in that it conduceth to the Service of the Former, and the preservation of the later. She therefore made this Heavenly Vertue judge of her Appetite; lest it should long after Excesse, the mother of all uncleannesse. Her Soule gave laws to her body; which it could not infringe, without the injunction of a strict Pennance. She devour'd Gluttony it selfe; and made the flesh subject to the command of the Spirit. Her fare, saith *Cedrenus*, required no vessell; nor need she to wash her hands, after her greatest meale.

Her dyet defide the fire, as of no ufe. From the Earths face, the Cows dugge, and the Fountains brimme, fhe readily fetched her fuftinance. She was as ignorant of the *Perfian* luxury, as the fuperftition. To this, her cloathing was correfpondent; for which, her backe was beholding to her fingers. Her hands were the purveyours to her other members. She had one eye fixed on *Heaven*, and the other caft upon the earth; being intentive on the Glories of the one, and the Neceffities of the other; and at once acted *Martha,* and *Magdalene.* It is very credible that fhe fowed, and fpunne, and maintain'd Life with labour. Hee Who gives life to all things, fuffer'd His then Adopted, and fince Naturall *Mother,* to gaine her living with fweat, and care, that her Example might give pride the checke, and teach Majefty Humility. In her, He made manifeft, that mortall Felicity is not the parent of the immortall. She was not folicitous for the feather, the looking-glaffe, or any outward bravery; being onely carefull to cover her fhame, and at once to

Her Infancy.

expell two deadly enemies to her Soule, and body, pride, and cold. Her outward Simplicitie was in all things anfwerable to her inward.

HER BETROTHING.

ELL, now she began to write woman; and her fifteenth yeare approached; and hand in hand with the increase of Time, went the acquisition of all Graces. Her least perfection, would render another most accomplisht. In her, all Vertues were at strife, all overcame. Nothing was here meane; she being no other, then an Union of superlatives. Charity, Obedience, Pietie, Virginity, all were, in her, at height. Nothing in her was wanting, but the DEITY It Selfe. Yet was not her vaineglory such, that she desired with *Dina* to visit the daughters of other *Regions*; and to enlarge the renowne of these her Excellencies; being onely studious in the Go-

Her Betrothing.

vernment of her owne little, inward *Common-Wealth.* Her fixed refolution was, not onely to confine her Perfon, but her Fame; which (had it penetrated forreigne *Countries*) *Kings* would have come fuppliants to her cottage; and on their knees, have petition'd for her love. But the bonds of her Matrimony were already afkt in *Heaven*; and no impediment found why fhe might not wedde GOD Himfelfe. Yet, at the earneft folicitation of the *Reverend Priefts*, faith *Mantuan*, was fhe content to be betroth'd to *Iofeph*; not that he fhould do the office of an Hufband, but ferve as a barre to the importunity of other Sutours; that fo fhe might the more freely enjoy, the inconceivable pleafure fhe tooke, in her vowed Virginity.

THE SALUTATION.

UT now, the time is come when she must be (to the astonishment of the world) a *Mother*, and yet remaine a *Virgin*. The Marriage betweene GOD, and Nature is concluded on in *Heaven;* and *Gabriel*, the *Ambassador* concerning mans Redemption, prepares himself for his journey, decreed from all Eternity. He receives instructions from the Hands of GODS Owne transcendent Mercy; and therefore, no doubt, but they are gentle, and pleasing. Clad in white, (as an Emblem of his Innnocencie) he sets forth without any other guard then his owne right Arme able to destroy *Legions*. The *Chaldæans* carried in their Ensignes a towring

Flame; the *Babilonians*, a Dove; the *Scythians*, Lightning; the *Persians*, a Bow, and Arrows; the *Romans*, an Eagle; and this extraordinarie *Ambassadour* of Peace, (being to descend from the higher to the lower world, from the CREATOUR to the creature, an *Angell* to men) beares along with him, in his very name, the signe of His Power, and Fortitude, that sends him. The gates, saith *Vernulæus*, of the Celestiall Pallace, stand wide open, and the Sacred TRINITY gladly beholds the departure of this Divine *Messenger*. The *Angels* clap their wings; and make the Heavenly Roofe ring with *Halleluiahs*. The *Saints* attend, and send their Vows after him, that his presence may be without terrour; and his sweet delivery, win consent in the heart of their glorious *Empresse*. The vaste space betweene the Poles is filled with troopes of Holy *Spirits*, who give a Convoy to this their fellow-*Servant*, graced above the rest, in having so important an affaire, as the Worlds Salvation, committed to his charge. The *Starres* put on new, and brighter aspects; as seeming to fore-

Vernulæus.

tell what they foresee not. The *Earth*, bedeckt with all imaginable ornaments, presents him with variety of sents, and colours even to her selfe new, and layes her prime dainties under his feet. Onely her stupid *Inhabitants*, whom his Embassie most concern'd, were altogether unsensible of his arrivall, and of the eternall Benefit he brings them; receiving him rather like an *Herald*, then an *Ambassadour*. And (which encreased his wonder at his entertainment) his first approach was unwelcome to the *Saint* whose Votary he was. He found her (as some thinke) alone; separated as well in body, as minde, from the world. She was not ignorant, that Piety was nearer pollution in society, than solitude; and therefore, to shun infection, she avoyded company. She well knew that the HOLY GHOST Himselfe had dwelt with the *Prophets* and *Apostles* in Caves, Dens, and Dungeons, and there pen'd the all-saving *Writ*. That which we call good-fellowship, and sweet conversation, her Conscience assured her to be, at best, but a sociable folly. In neighbourhood she

The Salutation.

feared proximity in vice. Well, if alone he found her, questionlesse she made a Divine use of that privacy, and meditated how in a corruptible body, to preserve a Spirit incorruptible.

The Celestiall *Agent* having demanded, and obtained Audience, spake the Oration he made not; for he was but *Interpreter* of the HOLY SPIRIT, in which Office he justly gloried. The Speech assuredly was modest; and sutable to the sacred eares it was to enter. The beginning of it, no doubt, consisted of a reverent applause of the perfections GOD had imparted to her. "*Haile*, Mary," said he, "*full of Grace*, "*the* LORD *be with thee: Blessed art thou* "*amongst women, &c.*" How she tooke this the Text following declares. "*And* "*when she saw him, shee was troubled at* "*his saying, and thought what manner of* "*Salutation that should be.*" No doubt the *Angell* no sooner pronounc't, "*Haile* "Mary *full of Grace*," but a blush arose in her bashfull face, and verified his words. But this colour was not fixed; it went quickly back, to fortifie her noble Heart,

[margin: S. Gabriel. S. Luke i. 29. S. Gabriel.]

against the feare that invaded it. She saw her selfe alone with One altogether a stranger to her, whose face she neither knew, nor his intent. True it is, his language was smooth, and even; but as faire words as these, have often proceeded from a foule heart. She trembled at his Salutation, thinking him to be a *man subject to abhorred lust, and therefore feared violence: but when she once knew him, and his Embassy, she then undaunted, discours'd with him as an *Angell*, whom before she quak't at as a man. I conjure all modest Soules that shall peruse this passage, by all things deare to them, to dwell long upon it, as worthily deserving both their Admiration, and Imitation. Though she received from him extreme, and Heavenly Praises, yet she was afraid, because she was alone. O Saviour of the World! Purity feares an *Angell*; shall not Impurity then suspect a man though in the shape of an *Angell*, when his complement,

---

* *That the* Angell *appeared to her in the form or shape of a man is the opinion of* S. Hierome, *in* Epist. ad Eustoch. de cust. Virgin. *and of* S. Ambrose, lib. 1. offic. cap. 18. *And that which* Damascen *hath,* lib. 2. de fide orthod. *All the learned approve of; to wit, that the* Angels *are transform'd, and appear to men according to the pleasure of the* Lord, *and reveale his divine Mysteries. And that* Angels *appear'd in the* Old Testament *in the shape of men is certaine: and for many reasons it is very probable that* Gabriel *assumed the form of a man when he came to the* Blessed Virgin. Chrysologus serm. 140, *is of opinion that the* Angel *appeared in a shape, and habit most pleasing and gentle, and that the* Virgin *was not troubled at his person, but his speech, in that it is said shee marvelled what sayings those should be.*

and discourse are sensuall. Virginity cannot bee too heedful, which makes it practise the doubt of things safe, that so it may accustome it selfe to the feare of things dangerous. If heathen women have, by nature, so abhorred pollution, that they have chosen death before it, how odious must we judge it to the Angellicall Innocency of GODS Owne *Mother?* Well, what course tooke she? She rejected these his Commendations, not with her tongue, but her lookes, which put on a dislike of all he had said. She had heard, that when Castles come to a parley, it is a signe of yeelding; and therefore thought it her safest way to involve her selfe within Humility, and a sober silence.

But the *Angell* quickly delivered her out of this Agony, into a greater; out of this feare, into a more tormenting care. " *Feare not* Mary," saith he, " *for thou* | S. Gabriel.
" *hast found favour with* GOD; *for loe!*
" *thou shalt conceive in thy Wombe, and*
" *beare a* SONNE, *and shalt call His Name*
" JESUS. *He shall be Great; and shall be*
" *called the* SONNE *of the* MOST HIGH; *and*

"*the* LORD GOD *shall give unto Him the Throne of his Father* David. *And He shall raigne over the house of* Iacob *for ever, and of His* Kingdome *shall be no end.*" To this her answer was, "*How shall that be, since I know no man?*" It is true, it is true, most Blessed *Virgin*, thou knowest no man; but let thy Modesty rest secure; for the Operation of GOD, and not of man, is here required. GOD should never be conceived in thee, wert thou not a *Virgin*; nor borne of thee, shouldest thou not remaine such. Thou canst not be spotted with the Conception, or Birth of an ISSUE so Immaculate. This feare is as needlesse, as that of defiling thy fairest fingers with the purest fountaine. If *Obededon* having received the Arke within his walles, was so enriched with all manner of Treasure, that Felicity was voyced to have descended from *Heaven* into his house; what shall we judge of thy supreme Blisse. O glorious *Virgin!* who art not to be the receptacle of a wooden Arke, but of His Only SONNE? With confidence, there-

The Salutation.

fore, confent to thy owne happineffe, and the Redemption of all Humanity.

But, indeed, I do not wonder at her aftonifhment, when I confider her bafhfulneffe. Meethinks I fee her, now cafting her eyes up to *Heaven*; now fixing them on the earth; and now againe on the *Ambaffadour* himfelfe, refolving to give up her Soule rather then her Virginity. Harfh muft the word (Conception) needs found to her who was a votary nere to know man; whofe onely love was Prayer; whofe onely childe was Piety. But when the *Angell* urged Gods Will, fhe forthwith yeelded a *Handmaid* to her Lords Defire. Let us intentively liften to the text. *" And the* Angel *anfwer'd, and faid* *" unto her, The* Holy Ghost *fhall come* *" upon thee; and the Power of the* Highest *" fhall overfhadow thee; therefore alfo that* *"* Holy Thing *that fhall be borne of thee* *" fhall be called the* Sonne *of* God. *And* *" behold thy* Coufen Elizabeth, *fhee hath* *" alfo conceived a fonne in her old age;* *" and this is the fixt moneth with her* *" who was called barren. For with*

_{S. Gabriel.}

"God *nothing shall bee impossible. And* "Mary *said; Behold the* Handmaid *of* "*the* Lord; *bee it to mee according to* "*thy word.*"

See here united, an incomparable Humility, and an Obedience even unto death. For the consenting to be the *Mother* of God, was not easie to her; in that a meek, and humble Spirit, with greater difficultie ascends the highest steppe of Honours Throne, then a proud, descends thence to the bottome; it being a thing in nature farre harder to climbe, then to come downe. If any man shall yet rest unsatisfied, and shall make a further enquirie after this difficulty, he may please to consider that her Humility ballanc't her Sonnes exalted, and her owne dejected, Estate; and as well meditated the care, the diligency, the reverence, and obsequiousnes, as the dignity, and excellency of her whom God would vouchsafe the most glorious Title of *Mother*. She wisely weighed, that the *Angels* were not worthy to wait on Him; and therefore the service of her whole life must as farre exceed, as the name of GODS *Mother* did excell that of *Servant*, or *Angell.* If *Saint Peter*, yet in the dawn of Grace, could so clearly discerne his MASTERS Greatnesse, as that he cryed out, *Depart from me a sinner*, as deeming himselfe unworthy of His Presence: If the *Centurion*, for the same respect, thought his house too base to receive Him; what should she thinke who was not to take Him into her ship, or her lodging, but into her Wombe, where He was to remaine not a Visitant, but a Dweller? Full well also she understood, that her consent was not onely required to be the *Parent* of the ALMIGHTY, but the *Spouse* also of His HOLY SPIRIT; to Whose Inspirations she ought a greater obedience then others, having received from the same SPIRIT a greater measure of Grace, and Honour. She clearly foresaw, that she was not onely chosen to conceive the SON of GOD, to bring forth, to nurse, and governe Him; but also, perforce, to yeeld Him up (such being the Divine Pleasure) to a *three* and *thirty yeares* persecution; and lastly to the cursed

S. Peter.

Many ancient Writers hold that she had the gift of prophecie.

Death of the Croffe, the Salvation of others depending on His Deftruction. And that fhe did forefee all this, plainly appeares by the fpeech of the *Angell* to her, who (after he had foretold the Conception, and Birth of CHRIST) added, *And he fhall be called* IESUS, that is, a SAVIOUR. [S. Gabriel.] An awfull reverence, and an inconceivable joy divided, without doubt, her all-holy Heart, when fhe contemplated her future, being a *Mother* to the MESSIAS. Can a man imagine any thing more difficult, more bitter for humane nature to overcome? Yet did her active Vertue vanquifh all thefe impediments, and with an humble, ravifht Soule, fhe expected the entrance of Him into her facred Wombe, whom already fhe had furely feated in her Heart.

Here, before we proceed to her Conception, we muft obferve two things not amply, and fully enough exprefs'd, very remarkable in the *Angelicall* Salutation; *Firft*, the dignity of the *Ambaffadour*; *Next*, the worth of her to whom his Embaffy was directed, together with her many

Vertues, equally eminent in this Divine Dialogue.

Concerning the *First*; he was not a man, but an *Angell*; neither an *Angell* of an inferiour *Order*, but of the supreme *Hierarchy*, which choise and pure *Spirits*, having received infinite Ornaments, and Graces from their Lord and Master, retained still His Favour, and ever stood before him. *S. Gregory* stiles him a principall *Angell*, treating of principall things. Some have not feared to call him the Supreme Angell, as *Damascen*, and others. Truth will answer for him, that amongst all the Celestiall *Spirits*, none are so predicated in Holy Writ as he, and *Michael*, to whom the Declaration, and Exposition of so high Mysteries so often were committed, as in *Daniel*, *Zachary*, and *Mary* is specified. Some will have his name to signifie God, and man; and that this Etymology containes a miraculous Mystery. Amongst these is *Proculus*, Arch-Bishop *of Constantinople*. " Geber," saith he, "*signifies man;* El, God, *alluding to* " *his Embassy, which treated of His ap-*

_{S. Gregory. Hom. 34. in lect. Evang.}

_{Damascen. Serm. de Virginis assump.}

_{Proculus. In 1 cap. Luc.}

"proaching birth, *Who was both* God
"*and Man.*" Saint *Bernard*, judgeth the
servant of *Abraham* to have beene a type
of *Gabriel;* for he was sent by his *Master*,
not to seek any *Virgin* that came next to
hand, but such a one as the Lord God
had prepared for the Sonne of His Lord.
"*This* Gabriel," saith Saint Chrysostome,
"*the Painters present to us winged; not*
"*that* God *created him so, but to denote*
"*the sublimmity and agillity of the Celestiall*
"*Nature, as also, to admonish us that,*
"*with gratefull hearts, wee acknowledge*
"*him to have for our cause descended from*
"*his highest habitation.*" And sweetly
Chrysologus; "*An* Angell *treated with*
"Mary *concerning our Salvation, because*
"*an* Angell *had dealt with* Eue *touching*
"*our damnation.*" This Blessed *Spirit*,
and *Saint Iohn* the *Evangelist*, *Damianus*
compares to two Lyons, which carefully
guard this our Sacred *Subject*. I will not
here seeke to satisfie the over-curious, and
needlesse doubts of *Luther*, and others,
whether she knew *Gabriel* to be an *Angell*,
or no; nor whether, or no, he entred her

The Salutation.

chamber the doore being fhut; nor whether he appear'd to her in a gentle familiar fhape, or in his full fplendour, as when he fo much amaz'd *Zachary*, and ftrucke him dumbe. Thefe queftions ferve rather to bufie curiofitie, then enflame Zeale. Neither hath all that tender fexe (to whofe good I dedicate this difcourfe) received an education that renders them capeable Iudges of fuch difputes. And I freely acknowledge, that in this Treatife, I have not fo much as ufed any one word not frequent, and familiar, becaufe I would make the fenfe cleare to the Femal Readers. Withall I profeffe my fcope is not to fharpen their wits, but to beautifie their lives; and to kindle in their faire bofomes, an holy Ambition to afpire to the perfections of that devout life, which this our incomparable *Lady* led, and ended with the applaufe of men, and *Angels*.

Laying afide therefore thefe fuperfluous arguments, I will proceed (as my method commands me) to deliver her ineftimable Worth, and fober Demeanour towards the *Angell*, which no eloquence can fo well expreffe as a filent, and reverent admiration. Much I need not fay of her, of whom I never can fpeake enough; efpecially having already produc'd fo many ancient, and learned extollers of her excellencies, to which my vote would adde no more then a dimme lampe to the glorious eye of *Heaven*, or an obfcure gloworme to a ftarry night. Yet fince at the Altar of this meek one (fweet and chaft as the Incenfe there daily burned) a fingle graine, fent from a fimple heart, is acceptable, I will not feare to pay her a due Oblation, though it come as fhort of her Value, as I of her Goodneffe. May it pleafe thee then, pious *Reader*, gratefully, with me to acknowledge that this is fhe who gave Flefh to Him, by Whom all flefh is fav'd. This was the *Dove*, that firft brought to us the Olive of our peace. This is the *Rainbow*, or firft *Signe* of our reconciliation to the Divine Majesty. And (to fhut up all in a little) this was the *Tabernacle*, and *Throne* of the Almighty, whence (His Majesty obfcured) His Love fhined forth to all Humanity. But in that, a plaine delivery of her Vertues adorne her more than can all the flowers of Rhetoricke; I will (though in an inelligant phrafe) fet fuch downe as fhall appeare moft eminent in this unparalell'd colloquy, wherein were handled the profound Myfteries of the Sacred TRINITY, as of the FATHERS Omnipotency, the HOLY GHOSTS Efficacy, the SONNES Excellency, and in Him the proprietie of both Natures.

HER PRUDENCY, AND HER OP-
PORTUNE SILENCE, AND
CAUTION OF SPEECH.

ER Prudency ſhall take the firſt place, not as the greateſt, but as the moſt diffuſive; becauſe cleane through this Dialogue it blends with all the reſt. Firſt, ſhe awfully, and adviſedly gives him full Audience; and at once, both obſerves the laws of Patience, and the cuſtome of good manners, in quietly attending the period of his Salutation. Many of her Sexe would have ſo cut him off at every word, that hee ſhould never have peec't his Speech together againe. Being more miſtreſſes of their tongues then their eares; they would never have given him hearing

Her Prudency. 43

till they had beene weary of talking. One of thefe, *Iuvenal* makes mention of in his 6. Satyre, who made a din able to free the Moon from the power of the Enchanter.

> *The common fort when the* Moone *was eclipfed thought her to be enchanted; and with bafons and other things made a hideous noyfe to barre her from hearing the charmers voyce.*

This Vertue of an opportune Silence few women obtain; if they do, it comes to them the laft of all other. Their tongues are clocks, which, once wound up, few of them go leffe then *fixteene houres.* But this wifeft of *Saints* in a feafonable filence, and caution of fpeech, was alike admirable: Infomuch that through the whole *Bible* we finde not that fhe fpake above *five* times. *Twice* to the Angell Gabriel, as " *How fhall this be?*" and againe, " *Behold the* Hand-maid *of the* Lord." *Next*, in the encounter betweene her, and her *Coufen Elizabeth.* A *fourth* time, to her Beloved Sonne, after long abfence, " *Why have you dealt fo with us.*" *Laftly*, when fhe becomes a Petitioner for the poore, " *Becaufe they have no wine.*" Here, in this place, fhe intentively hearkens to the *Angell*, whom fhe heares twice ere fhe replyes once. She

S. Luke i. 3, 4. 31.

S. Luke i. 46.

S. Luke ii. 48.

S. John iii. 3.

made two pawſes uſher her anſwer, which ſhe fram'd with ſuch care, and ſobriety, as if Modeſty had ſeal'd up her boſome, and lippes; and that without her ſpeciall warrant they were not to be opened. And though her thoughts were perplex'd and troubled, yet ſhe apparrell'd them in ſuch a cleare, ſmooth calme of language, that it would have gentiliz'd Barbariſme it ſelfe. When her Chaſtitie is call'd in queſtion, (which ſhe eſteemes above health, liberty, or life it ſelfe) ſhe poſitively denies nothing, in that ſtrange, and to her impoſſible aſſertion of the *Angell*; but anſwers, with an humble enquirie, "*How ſhall that be?*" Well might ſhe make this demand, ſince ſhe knew by humane power it could not be effected; and the *Angell* had not yet revealed, that ſuch was the Divine Will. Though never Soule endured a greater conflict then hers, and that feare had ſtretched the ſtrings of her heart to their utmoſt extenſion, yet choſe ſhe rather that they ſhould breake in ſunder, than ſhe into intemperancy. Some women (though chaſt, yet curſt,

Her Opportune Silence.

and hasty) having once heard their Chastity brought in question, would have omitted all interrogations; and have given the *Angell* a Sermon for his Salutation; and have reviled his Name, if not offered violence to his Person. But in this sweetest of *Creatures,* Mildeneffe and Modesty kissed each other; so that nothing could flow from her, that was not pleasing and gentle. Yet could not her amazed lookes conceale her feare, which afflicts farre more than griefe; for we grieve onely for what is past, but we feare all that can happen. The mercifull *Angell* reading, in her forehead, the perplexity of her Minde, resolved to ridde her of the tormenting doubt she was in; and to banish feare out of that face reserved only for Beauty, and the Graces to dwell in. He therefore hides this great Secret no longer from her; but expounds to her the manner, and meanes, of her Conception; which no sooner entred her eares, then consent her heart; and with a prostrate Soule she made her will conform it selfe to Gods; " *Behold, faith she, the* Handmaid *of the* LORD, *&c.*" In this confent of hers, we may difcover almoft as many Perfections as words. Some draw hence an obfervation, that the Salvation of mankinde depended upon her confent; and confequently the damnation, upon her refufall. My Meditation dares not climbe fo high; not being able to conceive how poffibly the Searcher of hearts fhould receive a repulfe from his Chofen *One;* nor how His Omnipotency can be confined to one onely Meanes, in the Redemption of mankinde. It fhall fuffice me, to derive hence three of the greateft Chriftian Vertues, her Faith, her Obedience, her Humility.

HER FAITH.

AITH is the hand whereby we lay hold on CHRIST, and His Merits, "*without which,*" faith *S. Auſtin,* "*all morall* [S. Auſtin.] "*Vertues whatſoever are no better than* "*gorgious ſins.*" The dignity and neceſſity of this ſupernaturall Gift, cannot but evidently appeare to the meaneſt underſtanding; in that no man is ignorant that without CHRIST we cannot be ſav'd; and without Faith, we cannot apprehend CHRIST, nor apply His Deſerts, and Paſſion to our polluted Soules. In this which excells all other perfections did this happy *Mother* of our EMANUELL, ſurpaſſe all other creatures, as here in briefe, and hereafter more at large, I ſhall demonſtrate. *S. Auſtin* both in knowledge and autho-

rity, infinitely exceeds me; and therfore I desire you would heare him for me. "*Strengthened by a singular Faith,*" saith he, "*she made* GOD'S SONNE *hers, more happy* "*truely in conceiving* CHRIST *in her minde,* "*then His Flesh in her Wombe. Endued* "*with this Faith she fear'd, and reverenc'd* "*Him whom she bore; Whom as soone as* "*shee brought forth shee ador'd, and was* "*the first beholder of the Glory of His Re-* "*surrection.*" Would I muster up my forces, I could produce many other Champions of the same worth, and antiquity; that with an indefatigable Zeale, doe vindicate the Faith of this Blessed *Virgin* against some of these latter ages, who accuse her as defective in that wherin she was most accomplisht. Their Objections have beene long since answer'd by *Saint Austin, Saint Ambrose,* and divers others of those Primitive times. *Saint Austin* distinguisheth thus betweene *Zacharies* demand and hers. "*Zachary when he* "*sayes, Whence shall I know this? or,* "*By what meanes shall I know this, I, and* "*my wife being so aged? he spoke this out*

S. Austin. Lib. de sanct. Virg. cap. 3.

S. Austin. Lib. 16. de civit. cap. 24.

"*of despaire, not by the way of inquisition.*
"*But* Mary *when she askes; How shall*
"*that be, since I know no man? shee utter'd*
"*this enquiring, not despairing. Where-*
"*fore to* Zachary *it is said, thou shalt be*
"*dumbe because thou believest not; but to*
"*her the cause is expounded, because while*
"*she doth question, she doubteth not of the*
"*promise.*" And to the same purpose, and almost in the same words speakes *Saint Ambrose*, whose testimony I omit, lest I should prove tedious, and obscure to the tender sexe, to whose profit this weake Essay of mine is chiefly intended. Yet my Zeale to her whose true Admirer I am, compels me briefly to deface all those aspertions, which the adversaries to her, and piety have layd upon her. And I am wholly transform'd into wonder, as oft as I consider how malice, and her spawne can bee so frontlesse as grossely to deprave the meaning of the Text, onely to detract from her; and should be so audacious, as to contradict the HOLY GHOST Himselfe, who by the mouth of *Elizabeth* pronounceth her Blessed, because she be-

[margin: S. Ambrose.]

leeved. True it is, their expofitions give a light to the *Scriptures*; but it is fuch a one as we receive from lightning, which brings with it rather terrour then comfort.

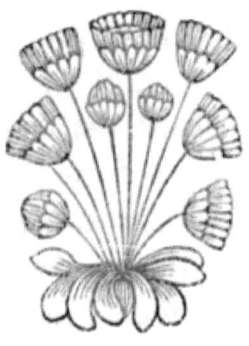

HER OBEDIENCE.

ERE her Obedience calls upon me to cut off, I cannot say, this digreſſion, but vindication of her Honour. Though ſhe deſerved ſoverainty, and command; yet delighted ſhe in nothing more, then in this ſubmiſſive Vertue, proper onely to a Subject; and was a diligent practitioner of it through her whole life, in imitation of Him who was obedient even to an ignominious Death. Her Faith, and Obedience were of equall ſpeed; for ſhe no ſooner heard the *Angell* relate that the ALMIGHTY had ordained, ſhe ſhould beare the worlds REDEEMER, but ſhe beleev'd, and conſented that it ſhould be ſo. She had learnt in her infancy, that Obedience, with GOD, is better then Sacrifice; and

therefore, ſhe was as ſwift as thought, in agreeing to the Divine Ordinance, that ſo poſteritie might diſtinguiſh betweene her Obedience, and that of others whoſe Wils, and Vnderſtandings have a combat before they can bee brought to a conſent. But this was onely a lovely branch of that beautifull Tree, her Humility, on which a perpetual Autumne attended; for it continually bore fruit.

HER HUMILITY.

F this Vertue I muſt treat more at large then of the reſt, becauſe it is extenſive cleane through all the actions of her life. Of this there are many ſorts, whoſe ſeverall countenances, and ſhapes we will here draw to the life; leſt the *Reader* be impos'd upon, and verily beleeve he enjoyes the true one, when, indeed, he is onely poſſeſſour of the adulterate.

We will begin with the Naturall Humility, which is to be found in many, who being baſely borne, and bred, and poorely ſpirited, aſpire not to greatneſſe, but reſt fully contented with that ſordid calling Fortune hath allotted them. This

Natural Humility.

Humility is none of those that Vertue doth warrant. There is *another* kinde which we may call Sensuall; and this makes men refuse Honours; not that they do not desire them, but for the trouble, care, and danger, that attended them. This Humility is base, and degenerate. There is a *third* proud one of the Hypocrite; who though he be ambitious of Dignities, and seeks them by all cunning, and undermining wayes, yet (to be reputed humble) he seemes to flie them. This Humility is false, and fained. A *fourth* there is Philosophicall, and Morall; and this consists in the knowledge of a mans selfe, and his miserable condition, so that by a naturall light he can see to humble himselfe, and be serviceable to all men; yet no further then the dignitie of his estate allows, and humane reason requires. So that, in this mans opinion, it should not be Humility, but baseneffe, in a Gentleman, to pardon an injury done him, or to place himselfe in an Hospitall as a servant to attend the sicke, and needy. This Humility will not endure the *Christian*

Sensuall Humility.

Hypocriticall Humility.

Philosophicall Humility.

Test. A *fifth*, *Mosaicall*, or *Iudaicall*, offers it selfe to our consideration; and this hath a neare resemblance of the true one; for by the perusall of the written Law we come to know our selves more perfectly then all the Philosophers of the world can teach us. To this purpose *Saint Paul* saith; "*From the Law comes the knowledge of sinne:*" and in another place, "*I had not knowne concupiscence to bee a sinne, had not the Law said; Thou shalt not covet.*" In this Mirrour we discerne our originall corruption, and all our disordinate passions, and affections, together with our ignorance, and frailty. By this Touchstone we finde all our moral philosophical Vertues to be but counterfeit. But this carries with it a very detrimentall discommoditie; for it leads us beyond hope of Salvation, and there leaves us. For when a man shall consider, that an unattainable Perfection, and an exact observance of the Law is required at his hands (wherein he is commanded to honour GOD with all his Soul, and with all his might, and to love his neighbour

Mosaicall, or Iudaicall Humility.

Rom. iii. 20.

Rom. vii. 7.

as himselfe) and yet withall shall discover in himselfe an utter disabilitie to execute these holy Commands; a frozen dijection wil so benumme all his thoughts, that not one of them will be of force, to uphold it selfe from sinking into the bottomlesse pit of despaire.

The true Christian Humility.

But with the true *Christian* Humilitie it is otherwise; which (having first made a submissive acknowledgement of its owne ingratitude, pride, avarice, injustice, impietie, and infinite other imperfections) by a strong apprehension layes hold on the Mercie of GOD in CHRIST. And this Goodnesse of GOD towards us, makes our sinnes more odious even in our own eies; no otherwise then the tender kindnesse of his Father, made the prodigall childe more clearly see his owne errour, and disobedience. For this makes that Speech of GOD to the *Iewes,* " *When* " *you come into the* Land of Promise, *then* " *you shall know your sinnes?*" as if He should have said, " *How often have you* " *distrusted Me, and not onely murmur'd* " *against Me, but abandon'd Me, and ador'd*

Her Humility.

"Idols, *making them your guides, and at-* *tributing to them the benefits you have* *received from Me?*" ſo the Regenerated *Chriſtian,* being once entred into the Spirituall *Kingdome* of CHRIST, ſees more clearly his ſinnes, then he did before his calling; as having received a greater Light. The excellency of this Vertue, in a *Chriſtian,* is beyond humane expreſſion. Not amiſſe a learned *Father* of the *Church* ſtiles this the Treaſurer of all other Vertues. The antient *Chriſtians* commonly uſurpe Humility for Vertue it ſelfe. CHRIST cals it Pooreneſſe of Spirit; and diſcourſing of mans Beatitude, ſets it in the front. This, and Pride are at endleſſe oddes; for this is ſociable, and loves company; wheras Pride affects ſolitude, and is for the moſt part alone. In the *Empire* of Pride, two cannot ſtand quietly together; whereas in the *Dominions* of Humility, an infinite number may be placed without either combat, or ſtrife. Pride is never void of feare, and doubt; whereas this ſtands ſecure with *Ionas* in the bottome of the Sea. Pride is ever

Hieron. in Epiſt. ad Celant.

ambitious of the first seate; this of the lowest; and therefore is as much extoll'd by all men, as the other cride downe. Pride assumes all to it selfe, and is full of selfe-love. This refuseth even its owne due, and undervalues it selfe; as knowing that it can justly call nothing its owne, but sinne. Pride stormes at an injury receiv'd; this embraceth all occasions that may exercise its patience. Pride (like all things puft up, and light) is wavering, and blown here and there by every gust of Fortune; this in stability is a Rock, not in hardnesse, being soft, and white as the Downe of Swans. Yet though this Vertue be of all other the most innocent, and submissive, it is withall the most powerfull; for, as *Nature*, so GOD abhors vacuity, and therefore (finding the humble utterly empty of affectation, presumption, and what else is derogatory to his honour) He fils him with His Grace and SPIRIT. What should I say more?

Humility is fearelesse, in danger; free, in bondage; rich, in poverty; quiet, in persecution; noble, and glorious, in ignominy; lofty, in lowneſſe; joyfull, in anguiſh; and happy, in the midſt of miſery. This made *Moſes* ſpeechleſſe; *Abraham*, to acknowledge himſelfe duſt and aſhes; *Iohn*, the *Baptiſt*, to eſteeme himſelfe a meer Voyce; and *Saint Paul*, to account himſelfe the greateſt of all ſinners. This Iewell was ſo faire in CHRISTS Eye, that to purchaſe it, He underwent not only poverty, miſery, and all indignities, but even execration, and malediction. What would we judge of a great *Prince*, who, in ſtead of enlarging his *Territories*, ſhould abaſe himſelfe ſo farre as to become a poore *Subject*? Why this did CHRIST, Who (being of all things the Greateſt, and Beſt from all Eternity) by Humility, became of all the Loweſt; and deſcended even to the profeſſion of ſervice to the meaneſt of His creatures. It is alſo an evident marke of His Humility, that He choſe to be borne of ſimple and obſcure Parents; whereas He might, if He would, have allyed Himſelfe to the greateſt *Princes*. This gave occaſion to the *Iewes* to mocke Him, ſaying, " *Is not* Ioſeph *His*

Father, and Mary *His* Mother?" True it is that He was of the *House* of *David*, but when He was borne, it was in its declination, and of no repute. As the Moone *fourteene dayes* together, to our sight, encreaseth; and *fourteene* againe diminisheth, till at length it be seene no more: so in the *fourteene* Generations from *Abraham* to *David*, the *House* of *David* received advancement in Honour, and Splendour, and was in his time at the full height; but in the *fourteene* following Generations it was in the wane; and in the dayes of CHRIST, neere utter extinction. And whereas he might have inserted *Sarah*, *Rebecca*, and many other *Saints* in His *Genealogy*; He placed *Tamar*, *Raab*, *Ruth*, *Bersabe*, and others of an incestuous race, to shew the world, that, though He hated sinne, He abhorred not sinners. What man is there who, having a lascivious wife, detected of whoredome, will take her againe? Yet CHRIST, having espoused the adulterate Soule of man, receives her into Grace and Favour, after she hath committed millions of adulteries.

[margin: S. John vi. 42.]

To this effect faith the *Prophet*, "*Though thou haft committed fornication with many Lovers, yet returne, and I will receive thee.*" Who is there that being injur'd will not onely forgive the Offendor, but feeke his friendfhip; I, and lay downe his life for him? All this did CHRIST, Who (being grievoufly and hainoufly abufed by man) not onely demanded his pardon, as if He Himfelfe had beene faulty; but made an Oblation of His Owne Heart-Bloud, to quench the Wrath of GOD, juftly conceived againft him. Another admirable Act of His Humility was, that (GOD having given Him all Power in Heaven and earth) in fo much that He could at His pleafure have deftroyed *Iudas*, whofe treafon He foreknew, all the revenge He tooke, was to wafh his feet, and to call him *Friend*, when he came to apprehend Him.

To thefe I may adde His living in obfcurity from His *twelfth* to His *thirtieth yeere*; in all which time we reade not any thing of Him. I will conclude with all the croffes and calamities He endur'd,

Jer. iii. 1.

of which in His Life He never reaped any fruit; and at His Death, had His Innonency onely predicated by one, and that one a *Thiefe*. In a word, during His Abode here below (whether you confider His Doctrine, Actions, or Paffion) He was not fo much delighted with the exercife of any Vertue, as of this gentle, meek one; that fo He might imprint it as His Owne Sacred Stampe, or marke in thofe mindes which He would have known to be His. And, above the reft, into the chaft Bofome of his deareft *Mother* did He fend this Divine Gift, before His Birth by infufion; and afterwards engrafted it there, by example. And this we may well perceive, by her fo clofely following the Patterne, that fhe precedes all but Himfelfe, in this milde, offenceleffe Vertue. In this rare Quality as fhe had an unequall'd Mafter, fo fhe prov'd a matchleffe *Schollar*. He who is ignorant of the excellency fhe hath attain'd to, in this one Perfection, I dare pronounce him withall, ignorant of GOD's *Holy Writ*, and incapeable of all Goodneffe derived thence. Yet

Her Humility.

some sacrilegious theeves there are, who robbe this beautifull *Temple* of its prime Ornament; this sweetest *Garland*, of its fairest Flower. They maintaine (me thinks the Earth should shake it selfe, and them when they utter it) that she was humbled, not humble. These I may more properly averre to be learning, not learned. They may with as much justice deprive the *Rose* of her blush; the *Lilly*, of her white; the *Violet*, of her purple; and the *Christall*, of its clearnesse; as her of this pretious Ornament, which she obtein'd by a studious pious Imitation, and preserv'd with a holy Care. But my wonder is the lesse, when I contemplate the continuall Antipathy betweene Impudency, and Innocencie. Whosoever shall settle his meditation on her discourse with the *Angell*; her Pilgrimage to her *Cousens* house; and her Divine Hymne there (though he have sworn himselfe the slave of prejudice) he will breake his chaine; and reassume so much freedome, as to declare her truly humble. Sure I am, if they would have her halfe a degree humbler, they make her wholly abject. To my thinking thefe *fixe* words alone (*Behold the* Handmaid *of the* Lord) are able to convince of errour *fix thoufand* fuch fhallow *Authors.* To thofe who are plac'd in an extreame height, all things below feeme farre fmaller then indeed, they are, but to themfelues they appeare the fame; but here it fals out otherwife, where the introducer of one pregnant Bleffing that contein'd all other into the world (and therefore worthily placed above it) thinks all things under her farre greater then her felfe, and above her in value. Certainly all the Ancient *Fathers* with one confent, affirme, that fhe deferv'd to be *Empreffe* of all others, who humbled her felfe below them all. For my owne part, I am fo tranfported with the meditation of her Meekneffe, that me thinks I heare her thus expreffing the humility of her fanctified Heart, to the Heavenly *Nuntio.*

S. Mary.
" *Is this a delightfull Dreame, or a*
" *pleafing Vifion that thus ravifheth my*
" *Soule? What a lovely profpect is this?*
" *What do mine eyes behold?* Cedars

Her Humility.

"*stooping to* Shrubs? Mountains *to* Vallies? *The* Ocean *courting a* Riveret? *I discover more than all this. I see* Heaven *descending to* Earth; *the* Supreame Majestie, *to* Humane Misery; *a Blessed* Angell, *to a wretched* Mortall. *True it is, I am the* Structure *of* Gods Owne Hands; *but an* Edifice *not cleare, not faire enough for the* Habitation *of His Onely* Sonne. *Alas, alas! I am a* Vessel *too uncleane to enclose a* Deity. *Is this Flesh of mine pure enough to clothe* Purity *It Selfe? I am not worthy to be reputed His* Childe, *much lesse His* Parent. *Oh lend me thy harmonious Voyce, thy Heavenly Rhetoricke, thou* Celestiall Oratour, *that I may render Him Thanks, and Praise; though not equall, yet nearer to the Grace I have received. I deny not but wee see His* Name *written in every thing here below, but in obscure Characters; like the discovery of the* Sunne *in a puddle. Thou art nearer Him in Essence, in Presence, in Goodnes, in Knowledge, and canst finde out words more suteable to His Worth.*

"*Wherefore I earnestly beseech thee, in thy best phrase, to present the unfained gratitude of his most humble* Handmaid, *who esteems her selfe unworthy to touch, much more to conceive Him. Neither shalt thou thy selfe depart without most humble thanks for the eternall Honour thou hast done me by this visit.*"

It is probable enough, she said much to this purpose; this forme of speech being agreeable to her disposition, and demeanour. To conclude this point, *six* cleare demonstrations of her Humility eminent above the rest, the *Holy Writ* offers to our serious, and reverend consideration. The *first*, in this submissive conference with the *Angel*. The *second*, in the house of *Zachary;* where the more her Vertue is predicated, by her *Cousen*, the more she humbles her selfe. The *third*, in her Delivery; where she meekly submitted her selfe to all wants, and inconveniences. The *fourth*, in her Purification; when she observ'd the custome of other uncleane, sinfull women, and rankt her selfe with them. The *fifth*, in

Her Humility.

Betrothing her felfe to a Carpenter; and in paying as great an obedience to him, as ever woman did to hufband, and in joyning with him in labour to get a poore living, to maintaine themfelues, and their SONNE. The *fixth*, in having a care of the poore, and in affociating them at all times. But of all thefe I fhall treate more at large in the courfe of this Divine Story, whofe order now brings me to the Myfticall Conception of her Bleffed SONNE, our Onely LORD and SAVIOUR IESUS CHRIST.

HER CONCEPTION.

HE Heavenly *Ambassadour* having executed his great Masters command, departs, leaves GOD, and Man in the Wombe, and the SONNE of Righteousnesse is now risen in the Virginall *Orbe*. For this is the* tenent of the True, and Ancient *Catholicke Church*, that she conceiv'd immediately after the *Angels* speech; whom I had rather follow, then accompany many of these later times, who oppose it. I will onely produce a few testimonies; and that of *Gregory* the *Great* shall be the Leader. " *The* Angell," saith he, "*declaring, and the* " SPIRIT *approaching, instantly the* WORD " *is in the Wombe; and presently in the* " *Wombe, the* WORD *is made Flesh, the*

* *This point is much controverted, and I leave it to the discreete Reader what to beleeve.*

S. Gregory. Lib. 18. Moral. ca. 27.

"*incommutable Essence coeternall to Him with the* FATHER, *and the* HOLY GHOST *still remaining.*" Him secondeth *Saint Austin*, of all the *Fathers* the most subtle and sollid. These ensuing are his owne words. "*When the* Angell *saluted the* Virgin, *then did the* HOLY GHOST *make her fruitfull; then did that* Woman *conceive a* Man *without a man; then was shee replenisht with Grace; then shee receiv'd the* LORD, *that Hee might be in her Who made her.*" And in another place he writeth thus. "*Make no delay, O* Virgin, *say but the word speedily to the* Messenger, *and receive thy* SONNE; *give thy Faith, and feele the Vertue of it.* Behold, *saith she,* the *Handmaid* of the LORD, *be it to me according to thy Word. Here was no delay at all; the divine* Agent *returneth; and* CHRIST *enters the Virginall Wombe.* The Mother of GOD *is suddenly made fruitfull, and is predicated happy throughout all ages. She presently conceived the* DIVINITY *of the* WORD *without the fellowship of a man.*"

S. Austin. De Symbol. ad Catechum.

S. Austin. Serm. 2. in festo Annun. Domin.

In this celebration of the Nuptials betweene GOD and Nature, while my affection advanceth one steppe, my reverence retires another. Here Reason is transformed into Admiration; Eloquence, into Silence. Some are rather solicitous to search into the profundity of the Mystery, than humbly to acknowledge it; and by Reason, seeke to pry into that which excludes all Reason. What was before time it selfe, is believed, not comprehended by man; for that transcends the understanding of man, which was before his Nature. No eyes but those of Faith, can penetrate this Wonder. All things in GOD are above Reason, nothing above Faith. Here, a *Virgin* conceives, without the losse of Chastity; a *Maide* remaines an Immaculate *Mother*. Eternity is here encompass'd by time;. Glory, masked in misery. A *Thing* finite containes Infinity; a *Mortall* encloseth Eternity. Here, the SONNE is as antient as His FATHER; elder than His *Mother*; and is made of her whom He made. Here is a concurrence, or a congregation, of Miracles. It is a Mira-

This Conception was predestinated before Time, from all Eternity.

Her Conception.

cle, that in the forming of such, and so great an issue, the aide of man should be utterly excluded; and that as He was Man, He was onely made of the pure Bloud of the *Virgin*. It is a Miracle, that the ordinary number of dayes, required in the forming of a humane body, is not here observ'd; but in a very moment without succession of time a Body is fram'd, and animated. But a greater Miracle than all these is, that at the same instant wherein the Soule is joyned to the Body; the Divinity, and Humanity are united in One PERSON, and the Eternall WORD is inseparably linkt with the Flesh; so that the SON of GOD, and Man is the same, in the *Virgins* Wombe. As for the manner of her Conception, I doe not more mervaile at the supernaturall strangenesse of it, then I doe at the daring inquisition, and sensuall expression of some, who relate it in words as grosse as their owne understandings. I only wish I could free the most learned, and ingenious *Eras-* [*Erasmus.*] *mus*, from the just imputation of a lascivious folly in the Essaying to unfold this sacred Myſtery. He compares God to a Woer; the *Angell*, to a Sollicitour; and *Mary*, to the Beloved; and proceeds further than either the Divine Will, or humane Modeſty permit. He treates of this venerable, this ſtupendious encounter betweene the Divinity and Humanity, in the ſame amorous phraſe with which the Poets deſcribe the wanton meeting of *Dido* and *Æneas* in the Cave. I will not rip up the particulars in which he is faulty this way; leſt I runne into the ſame errour which in him I reprehend, and imprint a bluſh on the cheekes of my baſhfull *Readers*. This Conception was as ſpotleſſe, and as cleare from all pollution as is a ſweet Odour when it enters the ſenſe. "*Here*," ſaith Saint Auſtin, "*the* Word *is the* "*Huſband, the Eare the Wife; in this glo-* "*rious ſplendour is the* Sonne *of* God *con-* "*ceiv'd; in this Purity, generated.*" Of the ſame cleare, and cleane ſenſe is *Rupertus* on this very paſſage. "*When the* "*truely believing* Maide," ſaith he, "*open-* "*ing at once her minde and mouth ſaid,* "*Behold the Handmaid of the* Lord, *be*

Marginalia:
Eraſ. in Annotat. Lei in Appendice ad Antapologiam Sutoris.

S. Auſtin. Serm. ii. in natal. Domini.

Rupertus, Lib. i. de operib. Spiritus Sancti. cap. 9.

"it to me according to Thy Word; *in
"the very instant (to make good the words
"of the* Angell) *the* HOLY GHOST *came
"upon her, and enter'd through the open
"dores of her Faith. What part did he
"enter? first the Chapell of her chaste
"bosome; then the Temple of her holy and
"incorrupt Wombe: Her bosome, that she
"might be made a* Prophetesse; *her
"Wombe, that shee might become a* Mo-
"ther."

Now for the time of this Conception; whether or no it were precisely on the 25. *day* of *March*, I will not strive to chaine any mans beleefe to a resolution herein; though I finde many old and great *Doctors* of the *Church* to have held it for a truth. Many questions here arise, which I have neither time, nor desire to discusse. I will onely looke into the deportment of this incomparable Creature, after that she knew she was become the receptacle of a DEITY. The meere apprehension of such an unheard of honour, in other women, would have begotten pride, arrogancy, and disdaine, not onely of all their sexe, but of mankinde it selfe. They would have repin'd at their breathing of common ayre; and (scorning the earth they trod on) have nourisht an ambition to walke on the battlements of *Heaven*. But this *Maide*, above imagination excellent, the more she was grac'd and dignified, the more she was humbled. When all men admir'd, and even ador'd her, and judg'd her worthy to be presently assumed into *Heaven*, she was ready to creepe into the center of the earth, and there to hide her; thinking that every one pointed at her, as undeserving that supreme Dignity confer'd on her by GOD Himselfe. And whereas others would have studied nothing but rich Tissues, and Embroyderies to weare; and the most costly *Persian* Carpets to tread on; she meditated simplicity in apparell, and a good paire of shooes to beare her afoot journey over the steepe and flinty *Mountaines*, intending to bestow a Visit on her *Cousin Elizabeth*.

HER VISITATION.

MANY ... high ... would ... ledg... ...d ; much lesse ... ...d dales, to make a ... ...ties ... them. Here is a ra... spectacle, Hu... lity climing, a ...ing as contrary ... ...ture of it, as it is ... things ... themselues to flie. ... ...er sexe, having the C... ...luded in the narrow ...ombe, made ha... ...ny, and rugge... her minde ... ...dy. And, ...uld she ... her

HER VISITATION.

ANY of her Kinde, and in her high Eftate, and Condition, would hardly have acknowledg'd, or receiv'd their kindred; much leffe have trotted over hils, and dales, to make a tender of their duties to them. Here is a rare fpectacle; Humility climing, a thing as contrary to the nature of it, as it is to things ponderous of themfelues to flie. This *Soveraigne* of her fexe, having the Celeftiall MONARCH included in the narrow compaffe of her Wombe, made hafte to paffe thofe fteep, ftony, and rugged hils; the willingneffe of her minde enabling the feeblenes of her body. And, to fay the truth, whether fhould fhe (whofe worth exalted her

above all things elſe) go but to places as eminent in ſcituation as ſhe in ſweetneſſe of diſpoſition? Whither ſhould this *Eagle* flie, but to the ſummity of the world? Sure I am ſhe could not ſore, above the pitch of her owne Value. Shee forſooke the ſweet embelliſht *Vallies,* where with eaſe ſhe might have walked; and betooke her ſelfe to the craggy *Mountaines,* which not without infinite labour, and paine ſhe could aſcend. By theſe rough, and uneven wayes, have the holy *Martyrs* themſelues mounted the *Promontory* of Vertue, and have found the end of their journey as ſweet, as their travell bitter.

The Author's addreſs to Virtue.

" O Vertue, *the minds that travell to*
" *thy* Indies, *how rich they returne! They*
" *come backe, laden with thoſe pretious or-*
" *naments, that beautifie this life; and*
" *thoſe* Panchayan *odours, that ſweeten the*
" *deprivation of it, and perfume poſterity.*
" *True it is that thy* Seas *are rough; & to*
" *him that lancheth into the deepe, appeare*
" *at firſt terrible; but if with confidence*
" *& conſtancy he plows them up, and with*
" *a fixed patience endures the frownes of an*

"angry Skie; he shall at length discover a
"calme, smooth as thy owne forehead, on
"which Fortune, Time, and vice could
"never yet imprint one wrinckle. Vnder
"thy sacred Safe Conduct, hath many a su-
"perstitiously devout distressed femall Pil-
"grim (after the endurance of heat, and
"cold without, of hunger, and thirst with-
"in, and other miserable accidents innume-
"rable) arrived with comfort at the sup-
"posed Shrine of this our Blessed Saint, who
"here (having no other guard than thy
"potent selfe) exposeth her dainty feet to
"the knowne cruelty of flints hard, and
"sharpe alike; and her Sacred Person to
"labour, and infinite hazards incident to
"the poore Traveller."

 She who meriteth to sit under a cloth of state, beset with the earths most precious stones, and a presence throng'd with *Empresses*, as happy waiters graced in this attendance, doth here commit her self into the hands of solitude, and danger. Thus did the *Spouse* of the HOLY SPIRIT overcome the narrow, and difficult paths of these steepe *Mountaines*; Charity leading her by one hand, and Humility by the other. And if we diligently peruse GODS Sacred Word, we shall there finde the *Mountaines* honour'd with many notable acts. Where did that parent of an innumerable issue, *Abraham*, prepare the immolation of his only sonne? On a *Mountaine*. Where did *Moses* receive the Tables of the Divine Law? On a *Mountaine*. Where did CHRIST, (His Humanity concealed) transfigure His Face into a Countenance of eternall Glory? On a *Mountaine*. Where did He shed His Purest Bloud; and lay downe His Dearest Life, as an expiation for our hainous and manifold sinnes? On a *Mountaine*. But why these famous Acts were performed on *Mountains* rather then in *Vallies*, Reason hath not a sight strong, and quicke enough to discover. But this is evident, that GOD hath not plac'd *Heaven* it selfe on the one side of us, or under our feet, but over our heads; that we might erect our looks, and fixe them on his eternall Habitation, and aspire to enter the Celestiall *Canaan*; indeed our true countrey, out of which while we live, we leade but a dying, and a flavish life, and are no other then unfortunate exiles. And surely, the very sight of sublime places, breeds in us high thoughts. We commonly looke downe on things despicable; the eyes of admiration are bent upward.

 The cause why she tooke this Journey, I shall endeavour to relate so briefly, that I will strive to avoid even long syllables. Yet do so many pious Doctrines, and Uses, flow from these two *Christalline* Springs, that they alone are sufficient to compose an entire Booke of a vast volume.

 The *Angell* that he might beget, and strengthen a beleefe in *Mary* of what he had said, confirms this Miracle with another, and tels her that her *Cousen Elizabeth*, also in her old declining age, had conceiv'd a sonne, and that this was now the *sixth moneth* of her being quicke. These glad tydings, no doubt, delighted much our Blessed *Ladies* Minde; where they could not stay without rendring a faire encrease of Fruit, first in meditation, then in action. Questionlesse, she no sooner heard them but her Soul was delivered of a twinne of Vows; the first was, to praise GOD, that He out of his best Pleasure, and infinite Goodnesse had vouchsafed to crowne her *Cousens* fruitfull Vertue with the Blessing of a childe, she being now in *yeares*, when despaire had chased all such hopes out of her breast, and barrennesse (as the world conceiv'd) had seal'd up her Wombe. The other was, all impediments set apart, to give her *Cousin* a visit in her owne *Country*, and habitation. Having performed the first, her thankesgiving for her, she undertakes the latter, her journey to her. Nor was she long about it; but with all speed possible set forward, lest she might seeme not readily to obey the Incitation of the HOLY GHOST; or be wanting to her *Cousin* in any good office shee could doe her. Neither could the consideration of her owne Majesty, of the teeming Estate she was in, of the disasters to which *Travellers* are subject, of the unevennesse of the way, or of the* length, (which *Melancthon* affirms to have beene *twenty Dutch miles*) deter her from un-

---

In concione de visitat. Mariæ.
* *From Nazareth to* Ierusalem, *where that* Elizabeth *dwelt, not onely many moderne* Divines *but* S. Austin, *and* Beda *affirme.*

Her Visitation.

dergoing this tedious Pilgrimage. And as she readily undertakes it, so she makes haste in it. She well understood that delayes in Spirituall affaires were as dangerous as relapses in bodily diseases.

HER CHARITY.

EHOLD here a prodigall Charity that hath no refpect of it felfe, being onely intentive on the good of another. It was Charity, that withdrew her from her beloved privacry, into the publike view, which till then fhe had ever fhun'd. It was Charity, that added wings to her feet; and armed her Heart againft all finifter accidents that could happen. It was Charity, that emboldened her to goe to her *Coufin* without any invitation, not being expected by her, or, happily, by face knowne to her, and with confidence of welcome to enter her houfe. It was Charity, that caus'd her to tender fervice there, where it was due to her felfe. It

Her Charity.

was Charity, that cheer'd her up, and sent her on this congratulating Embassy. Lastly, it was Charity, that invited Sanctity it selfe enclosed in this happy *Maide*, to hasten to the Sanctification of the childe in the wombe of *Elizabeth*.

Having patiently passed the troubles and annoyances of her Voyage, she with joy at length arrives at her *Cousins* Habitation; into which she no sooner puts her head, but the Reverend *Prophetesse* (having no other Revealer, nor Prompter than the HOLY SPIRIT) immediately knoweth the *Mother* of her LORD to be there present; and knowing, doth acknowledge it; and acknowledging, doth magnifie her Perfections; & professeth her House blessed in being graced with her vouchsafing to be in it. She, at first sight, discernes in her so many, and so great concealed Vertues and Mysteries, that a man would judge she had beene present at the enterview of her, and the *Angell*. Nor did she conceale these her Excellencies; but did describe them with such Skill and Zeale, that Fame was even proud to repeat them.

Could the domesticall servants, thinke you (having heard their *Mistresse* predicate her Divine Qualities, and transcendent Condition) containe themselves from divulging a joy, which a narrow humane bosome is not capacious enough to receive? Could they abstaine from justly boasting, that a beauteous, Blessed *Maide* resided then in their House, which together with their Soules, were, by her glorious presence, enlightened?

But I can no longer with-hold my pen from setting downe the Journey it selfe, and their mutuall Salutations in the same words, wherein the *Text* commends them to us. "*And* Mary *arose in those dayes,* "*and went into the* Hill-Country *with haste* "*to a* City *of* Iuda, *and enter'd into the* "*House of* Zacharias, *and saluted* Eliza- "beth. *And it came to passe as* Elizabeth "*heard the Salutation of* Mary, *the Babe* "*sprang in her belly, and* Elizabeth *was* "*filled with the* Holy Ghost: *and she* "*cryed with a loud voyce, and said:* "'*Blessed art thou amongst women, because* "'*the* Fruit *of thy Wombe is Blessed.*

S. Luke i. 39.

S. Elizabeth.

Her Charity.

"'And whence commeth this to paſſe that
"'the Mother of my LORD ſhould come to
"'me? For loe, as ſoone as the voyce of thy
"'Salutation ſounded in mine eares, the
"'Babe ſprang in my belly for ioy. And
"'bleſſed is ſhee that believ'd; for thoſe
"'things ſhall he performed which were
"'told her from the LORD.' Then Mary *S. Mary.*
"ſaid; ' My Soule magnifieth the LORD,
"'and my Spirit reioyceth in GOD my SA-
"'VIOUR; for He hath regarded the low-
"'lineſſe of His Handmaid; for behold from
"'henceforth all generations ſhall call me
"'Bleſſed. Becauſe He that is Mighty hath
"'magnified me, and Holy is His Name.
"'And His Mercy is from generation to
"'generation on them that feare Him. Hee
"'hath ſhewed Strength with his Arme,
"'He hath ſcattered the proud in the ima-
"'gination of their hearts. He hath put
"'downe the mighty from their ſeates;
"'and hath exalted the Humble and
"'Meeke. He hath filled the Hungry
"'with good things; the Rich He hath
"'ſent empty away. He hath upholden
"'Iſraell his Servant, being mindefull of

"'*His Mercy. As He hath spoken to our Fathers, to wit*, Abraham, *and his* Seed *for ever.*'"

In this Salutation of *Elizabeth*, the springing of the Babe in her wombe at the sound of our sweetest *Ladies* Voyce requires, not only our Observation, but Astonishment. He that was greater than all the *Prophets*, as yet not borne, and enclosed in the narrow compasse of the wombe, no sooner heard the charming Voyce of this Heauenly *Nightingale*, but he leaped for joy, essaying then, and there to exercise the Office of the *Fore-Runner* of his *Master*. The Asseveration of some, that this was not an effect of the *Virgins* Vertue, but of the WORD Incarnate, may be admitted for good, if we onely have an eye to her Vertue, and exclude the aide, and power of the Divine Grace. But all Wisedomes Children are by Truth her selfe informed, that many things are lawfully attributed to secondary Causes, the primary and efficient Cause not rejected. And this way we may impute to *Mary*, what worke soever GOD, with her co-ope-

S. Bernard saies, that if an Infant was so over-joyd at the sound of her voyce, what will the joy of the Celestiall Inhabitants be, when they shall see and heare her? Serm. 1. de Assump. Mariæ.

Her Charity.

rating, hath wrought, either in the House of *Zachary*, or else where, for the benefit, and instruction of us poore mortals. Neither will any sound, and sollid judgement attribute any thing to the conspicuous Merits of the *Virgine Mary*, or any other *Saint*, without the concurrence and predication of the Divine Grace; who by those *Saints* that serve, and feare Him, distributes His Gifts, and Favours to Mankinde. That Sentence of CHRIST is no way obscure; " *He that beleeves in Me,* " *shall do the Works that I do, and greater.*" By many examples, the *Scriptures* do confirme the comming of *Saints* to any mans dwelling, to conferre upon him both Grace, and Happinesse. *Three Angels* came to *Abraham*, Whom he entertain'd taking Them for *Pilgrims*, when the *Patriarch* forthwith became fortunate in the obteining of that for which so long he had offer'd up vows to GOD, namely a sonne; his wife and he, being by the course of Nature, past the generation of children. Againe, *Two Angels* came to *Lot*, and lodg'd in his House at *Sodome*, and sav'd their Host, and

S. Iohn xiv. 2.

Gen. xviii. 2.

Gen. xix. 1.

his *two* daughters from being reduc't to cinders with their *City*. *Iacob* visited wicked *Laban*, to whom God granted a singular Blessing for that idolater, in so much that he himselfe confessed it, saying, " *I learned by experience, that* God *hath* " *blessed me for thy sake.*" *Elizeus* to expresse the kindnesse he received at the hands of his Hostesse, the *Shunamite*, restored her dead sonne to life. The *Apostles* themselues brought Peace, and Felicity to all hospitable men whose dwellings they enter'd. And shall the arrivall of Gods Owne *Mother* at the House of *Zachary* prove onely vaine, and fruitlesse in bringing no Divine Consolation to her kindred? Yes surely, *Elizabeth* tasted the fruit of her all-gladding Presence; for she could not conceale the pleasure conceived in her Heart, but utter'd it in the best words she could. *Iohn* himselfe also, rellisht it, and by his motion gave what signes he could of the content, and worship he receiv'd, and pay'd. Neither could it otherwise be, but the Mansion of *Zachary*, and the adjacent *Countrey* were both

Gen. xxx. 27.

2 Kin. iv. 35.

Her Charity.

delighted, and sanctified, by the *three moneths* residence of her, who bore not about, but in her, the AUTHOR, and CONSUMMATOUR of all Piety. Their joy, questionlesse, was beyond imagination great; in that they had never before seene GODS Gifts, and Graces passing through so pure an *Organ* of His SPIRIT. But the aged *Prophetesse* herselfe, doubtlesse was in a holy, delitious Trance, at the very *first* steppe she made over her threshold; and thought her House but halfe blest, till the other foot was in. Their mutuall Salutation surely was low, and submissive; which I cannot better expresse, then by the supposition of the encounter of *two* shades, softly creeping ore the face of the earth. The *Evangelist* delivereth onely the Compendium of their Conference; which could not be but as long as serious. They treated surely, of deepe Miraculous Mysteries; as of the Incarnation of the WORD; of the Persecution of her, and GODS Onely SONNE; as also of His Passion, and the Salvation of Mankinde. And here it will neither be a thing impious, nor imperti-

Life of the Blessed Virgin:

nent (binding our selues strictly to the substance of their short Discourse) to ayme at the amplification thereof; by which happily, it may come to passe, that the supposition of what they might say, may turne to a Truth of what they said indeed. This then, or like to this, was, or might be, the speech of the holy Matron to the more Holy *Virgin:*—

S. Elizabeth *to* S. Mary.

"*What looks shall I put on? What words shall I assume, what entertainment shall I finde out, O Princely Virgin! to give thee a welcome answerable to thy merits, who art Superiour, to the Saints in Heaven, and the prime glory of thy Sex on Earth? I am wholly transformed into shame, when I consider every way thy Excellency, and my unworthinesse. Alas! what is there in miserable me, that should invite the* Mother *of my* LORD, *to afford me a visit, who am the meanest of His Creatures? What equality is here? Thou who art full of Grace, comest to mee void of it. Thou who art famous for thy Fertilitie, to me who have beene a long time infamous for my Barren-*

Her Charity.

"neſſe. Thy Charity, and Humility made
"thee forget thy ſublime, and my low eſtate,
"and conducted thee to my poore Cottage,
"no way fit to receive thee. Moſt of thy
"Sexe having attained to thy ſupreame Con-
"dition (who did'ſt conceive and nouriſh the
"CREATOUR and REDEEMER of the world,
"with that thy cleareſt Bloud of which He
"was made) would have advanced their
"heads above Mortality, and diſdaining
"all inferiour Converſation; would have
"demanded as their due, to be aſſumed into
"the Imperiall Heaven. But in thee, one
"heat hath expelled another; the flames
"of thy Zeale have utterly conſumed thoſe
"of thy Pride (if any thou ever had'ſt);
"and thou art ſo farre from vaunting, that
"thou by all meanes ſeekeſt to conceale that
"daintie Fruit, of which all Poſterity ſhall
"taſte, and never be ſatisfied, and for which
"all Generations ſhall call thee Bleſſed.
"But from others thou mayſt hide it; from
"me thou canſt not; to whom the SPIRIT
"hath reveal'd it, and the ſpringing of
"the Childe in my wombe, hath teſtified it;
"and if the Children of Iſrael ſhould be ſo

"dull, and unhappy, as not to apprehend
"it, GOD would give the stones an articu-
"late voyce to proclaime it. The LORD
"of mee, and all things else, hath firmely
"seated Himselfe in thee; and chosen thee
"for His Mother, to the end that the Seed
"of Abraham may breake the head of the
"Serpent; and the Sonne of David bring re-
"liefe to his forlorne and distressed Church,
"streightly beseiged by the Prince of Dark-
"nesse, and his infernall Troopes. True
"it is, I am above thee in yeares; but in
"desert, infinitely below thee, and therefore
"ought to have prevented this thy painfull
"journey by comming first to thee, to con-
"gratulate thy happinesse; and not onely
"in the behalfe of my selfe, my Kindred,
"and Nation, but in the Name of GODS
"selected People, to tender thee most hum-
"ble, though not condigne, thanks for so
"readily assenting to beare, bring forth,
"and educate their Soveraigne LORD and
"REDEEMER. But thou, having gotten
"the start of me in Goodnesse, art come to
"me, ere I could set forward towards thee;
"and now thou art here, I repine at nothing

" *more than at my disability to serve thee.*
" *Thou who meritest to have the* Earth,
" *the* Water, *and the* Ayre *ransack't, to*
" *please thy pallat, shall have nothing here*
" *but the simple viands of* Nature, *prepared*
" *by as simple an* Art. *But trust me, what*
" *ever is here is truly thine owne, and my*
" *selfe to boot. My willing Heart to waite*
" *on thee, and obey all thy Commands, shall*
" *supply all other defects. Such is my de-*
" *sire to attend, and please thee, that doe*
" *but signifie thy pleasure by the least becke*
" *or nod, and thou shalt see how nimbly I*
" *will bestirre these aged limmes; and place*
" *before thine eyes, a plaine and evident*
" *conversion of* Impotency *into* Ability. *I*
" *shall not thinke any paines, my weakenesse*
" *can endure too great, nor any cost my purse*
" *can compasse, too deare for thee. Wher-*
" *fore, I earnestly beseech thee to blesse me,*
" *and my House with thy long abode; and*
" *let not our course and slender fare make*
" *thee hasten my death, in thy sudden re-*
" *turne. O my brightest* Starre! *envy me*
" *not thy comfortable shine; but let me* Live
" *in it, till I exchange it for a brighter in*

"Heaven. *The dayes of my Pilgrimage
"are even now at an end; O leave me not
"then, who art the* Staffe *and* Solace *of
"mine Age! but stay the arrivall of my last
"minute, and with thy fairest hands close
"up these my dimme eyes. So shall I bid
"farewell to this world with content, and
"enter the other with Glory. Thou, my
"sweetest* Princesse, *who hast verified the*
"Prophecy *of* Esay; *and being an un-
"spotted* Virgin, *dost conceive and bring
"forth to the world our* Emanuell; *grant
"this my first, and most humble request. O
"thou* Daughter *of* Abraham! *who hast
"surpassed thy* Fathers Faith, *in beleeving
"things which seeme more impossible to hu-
"mane Reason: if in this rude speech of mine
"I have over-talked my selfe, or under-spoken
"thee, impute it to my declining and doting
"yeares, and grant me thy Pardon. Thus
"I end; but not without adding to those I
"have already given thee, a Myriade of
"Welcomes, and a Million of* Aves *more.*"

The Vertuous *Maid* undoubtedly was not here mute, but devided her speech betweene God, and her *Cousin.* She di-

Her Charity.

rected (with I know not whether greater Piety, or Prudency) her Praife to the Former, ere fhe would vouchfafe to make a reply to the latter. An anfwer without all peradventure her Humanity afforded her, and to this purpofe for ought we know, might it be:—

" *Deareſt* Coufin, *your own Wifedome* [S. Mary to S. Elizabeth.]
" *will plead my excufe, in that I rendred*
" *Him Laud to Whom it belongs, ere I ac-*
" *cepted of it my felfe, to whom it is not*
" *due. You magnifie me; and I, my* CREA-
" TOR. *Your Sacred Iſſue moved with de-*
" *light at the found of my harfh Voyce, and*
" *my Spirit rejoyceth in the Mercy of my*
" *Sweeteſt* SAVIOUR. *You give me Attri-*
" *butes more proper to my* MAKER *than to*
" *me; not unlike thofe* Heathen *who take*
" *off the heads from the Images of their*
" Gods, *and faſten them to the fhoulders of*
" *their* Princes *Statues. Your commenda-*
" *tions fit your felfe better than me; and*
" *refemble thofe refplendent Rayes which*
" *returne into the radiant body that fent*
" *them forth. In a word, you have fub-*
" *fcribed my Name to your owne Character.*

"The humbling and undervaluing of your
"self, is a strong argument of your Vertue;
"for as in a field of Corne we see the empty
"eares to hold up their heads, the fuller to
"hang them downe. I am in my Spring,
"you in your Autumne; I produce the
"Blossome, *but you beare the Fruit.* What
"the most penetrating Eye can discerne in
"me; the most partiall Tongue will call a
"superficiall ornament; but the dimmest
"Sight may soone discover that in you, which
"the most detracting Penne must be forced
"to style essentiall Worth. Thus dignified,
"give me leave to tell you, sweetest Cousin,
"that you offer me an Affront together with
"your Service. A seemely sight it were
"surely to behold decrepit Age waiting on
"active Youth; wisedome on Vanity; a
"venerable Matron on a simple Girle. The
"scope of my journey is to attend you; to
"lend you my Strength, now your owne failes
"you; and to serve you, through all the
"offices of your Hand-maid. Doe but in-
"timate your Will by the least signe, and
"you shall see me flye to performe it. Your
"Invention cannot devise any thing so im-

"possible, which my Will (ambitious to
"please you) will not judge most easie to be
"executed. Whereas you entreat me to
"stay long with you, you transgresse the
"Lawes of Friendship in petitioning her
"whom you may justly, and boldly command.
"A thing strange to me it is, that you should
"thinke me so stupid, and sencelesse, as that
"I should need an Invitation to be made
"truely happy. Before I had the honour
"to see you, I envied those that enjoyed
"your sweet and Divine Conversation; and
"thought they enricht themselves with my
"losse; wherefore a Staffe to beat me hence,
"is more requisite, than Oratory to keepe
"mee here. Ever since the Blessed Angell
"imparted to me the Newes of your being
"fruitfull, my desire to see you hath beene
"restlesse; and next to God, I have onely
"meditated you, and your Goodnesse. O
"my best Cousin! whose fervent and de-
"vout Prayers obtaine Victories; whose
"Fasts, Abundance; joyn with me in
"Thankesgiving to God, for the Grace
"which I shall never be able to conceive,
"much lesse to expresse, or deserve. Him

"*with all my Heart, and with all my*
"*Soule I invoke, that Bleſſings may fall*
"*upon you before, and above your Wiſhes;*
"*and that you may yet long live to His*
"*Glory, and my Comfort.*"

Had their *three months* demeanour each to other, together with their Godly diſcourſe, and pious practiſe of it, beene penn'd to poſterity (had all other *Bookes* been burnt, ſave that and the Bible) the Femall Sexe in theſe *two* ſhould have found matter ample enough to exerciſe both their Meditation and Action. Sure I am the *Romiſh Church*, as in an honourable memoriall of this their Charitable Encounter, hath ordained the *Annuall Celebration* of a ſolemne *Feaſt*. And the *Councell* of *Baſil* (of what Authoritie in other things I know not; certainly in this one particular, very commendable) hath decreed the Solemnization of this *Feſtival-Day* in theſe verie words.

<small>Seſſ. 43. Concil. Baſileen.</small>

"*The* Bleſſed Virgin *being inſtructed*
"*by the Celeſtiall* Meſſenger, *and conducted*
"*by the* Holy Ghost, *aſcended in haſte*
"*the mountanous* Countrey, *and entred the*

"humble House of Zachary. For Iesus
"who was in her Wombe, made haste to
"blesse Iohn as yet in his Mothers Belly.
"And the most Glorious Virgin visiting her
"Cousen Elizabeth, was pleasing to her
"both in her loving Visitation, and fruitfull
"Colloquie. The Consideration of this Ex-
"celling Mystery ought to delight the mindes
"of the Faithfull, wherein these two glo-
"rious Mothers (who bore about them the
"commencement and accomplishment of our
"Salvation) did so familiarly communicate
"their joyes, and wherein the most excel-
"lent Virgin Mary of the House of Da-
"vid, and Elizabeth the most venerable
"amongst the Daughters of Aaron discours'd
"together. The first of these had inclosed
"in her Wombe the Creatour and Re-
"deemer of us all; the latter, his Fore-
"runner. These Saints being made Mothers
"by a Miracle, conferr'd together of the
"Divine Benefits they had received. The
"meeting of this worthy paire was most
"happie, and illustrated with great, and
"glorious testimonies of the Divine Grace.
"The one conceived by the cooperation of the

" Holy Spirit; *the other by Myracle in*
" *her old Age, and both their Issues foretold*
" *by the Celestiall* Angell. Iohn *as yet*
" *imprisoned in his Mothers wombe doth*
" *worship his* Lord *borne to him in* Maries
" *Belly; and* Elizabeth *fill'd with the*
" Holy Ghost, *doth Congratulate the*
" *Conception of the* Sonne *of* God, *and the*
" Saviour *of Mankinde; and prophecying,*
" *declares her* Cousen *blessed in beleeving,*
" *and contemplating the Mysteries revealed*
" *to her.* On the other side, Mary, *full*
" *of unutterable joy, layed up all these say-*
" *ings in her heart, which before she had*
" *heard from the* Angel, *and now from*
" Elizabeth, *and breaks out into a Song of*
" *Thanksgiving to the* Lord. *Who can*
" *sufficiently praise so great Mysteries?*
" *Who can declare those Joyes to the*
" *full?* Iohn *not yet borne rejoyceth;*
" Elizabeth, *is delighted with the arri-*
" *vall of the* Virgin. Mary *is extreamely*
" *pleased in the Mysteries; the* Saviour
" *of the World is acknowledged by His*
" *Fore-runner; not onely the* Angels, *but*
" *Heaven and* Earth *resent the pleasure;*

"*and the Whole* TRINITIE *is glorified with
new praises. Wherefore the greatnesse
of these joyes is to be extolled with espe-
ciall commendations, and with singular
solemnities to be celebrated; and the* LORD
in the Wombe; the Virgin *that beares
Him; the Barren that conceives; and the
Fore-runner that it sanctified, ought to be
presented with all imaginable praises and
honours.*"

With this pious and gratefull Ordinance of the *Church*, I conclude the Visitation of our incomparable *Lady*, and now proceed to her Deliverie.

HER DELIVERY.

WE reade in *Holy Writ* of *three* ſupernaturall Productions, the one of *Adam*, the other of *Eve*, the laſt of CHRIST; which as moſt Miraculous we are now to treat of. Here in his *Nativitie*, as before in his *Conception*, let us turne *Inquiſition* into *Thankſgiving*; and with one Spirit and voyce ſing aloud, "*The* Stone *which the Builders refuſed is the Head of the corner. This was the* LORDS *doing, and it is marvellous in our eyes. This is the day which the* LORD *hath made; let us rejoyce, and be glad in it.*" This is our wedding-day, wherein by the SONNE, we are joyned to the FATHER. This is the day of the new Union, wherein He Who is GOD, re-

Ps. cxviii. 22.

maineth the same that He was, yet for our sakes is borne, and made what He was not; wherein He that was every where without a Body, is made present to us by a Body, that what GOD hath by *Nature*, men might receive by *Grace*. This is a great, a joyfull, a fortunate, a desired day, the end of the Law, the end of the *Prophets*, the beginning of the *Gospell*, nay the *Gospell* it selfe. This is a day of State, usher'd by the *Angels*, follow'd by the *Apostles*. Let our Mindes remove the distance of time and place, and dwell a while with our All-Holy LORD and Blessed *Lady*, lest we loose the pleasure of this day, the least accident whereof is Mysterious. What a brave assembly of Visitants of all conditions, resorted this day to this place, which then might rightly be called the *Randevous* of the *Saints*? Would you see those who are above men, but below Him who is borne? Behold the *Angels* singing His Birth. Do you desire to behold the Married? Here you have *Zachary* and *Elizabeth*. The Unmarried? Here you have *Symeon*. Widdows? Here you have *Anna*.

Priests? Here againe you have *Zachary.* Wise men? Here you have them from the *East.* Ideots? You have here the *Shepheards.* But here is to be noted, that these keepers of beasts heare the voyce of the *Angels* before any of the other, first receive the *Gospell,* and first divulge it. And in this they were more happie than *Augustus* himselfe, who (though he had made a firme Peace by *Sea* and *Land,* and had now the *third* time shut up the *Temple* of *Ianus*) yet was he ignorant of the Blessed Peace concluded on betwixt God and Man.

O how much sometimes Ignorance avails in Divine Matters! *Kings, Potentates,* the *Rulers* of the *Earth,* and the Wise of this world are asleepe while Christ is borne. These most simple of Mortals, and innocent as the creatures they tend, watch all night; and therefore are first made partakers of these joyfull news. As their owne wooll, not yet dipt in any dye, readily drinks in any colour they please to bestow on it: so their minds voyd of all humane Wisedome, greedily suckt in the Divine; Faith is the *Compendium* of Salvation;

and humane knowledge of times, the obstacle of Faith. *Ariſtotle* having confined to *Heaven*, the Maker, and Moover of it, would never have beleeved His Birth here below. *Plato* would have derided this Miraculous relation, who the more he attributed to GOD, the leſſe would he have expected His ſo humble comming into the world. Neither would the *Stoicks* who held GOD to be a Fire; nor *Hipocrates*, who thought Him to be a Warm'th, ever have look't for Him clad in Fleſh and Bloud. Wherefore they are here elected Witneſſes of this ſtrange Truth, whoſe Science was of ability ſtrongly to beleeve, not wittily to diſpute. O what proficients in Faith did theſe ruſticall Swaines prove in a moment! What a profound ſecret is imparted to them? Let us examine the verity of this by that infallible Touch-ſtone, the text.

" *And there were in the ſame* Country, S. Luke ii. 8.
" Shepheards *abiding in the field, and keep-*
" *ing watch by night, becauſe of their*
" *flocke, and loe the* Angell *of the* LORD
" *came upon them, and the* Glory *of the*
" LORD *ſhone about them, and they were*

Life of the Blessed Virgin:

The Angell.

"sore afraid. Then the Angell said unto
"them, 'Be not afraid; for behold I bring
"'you tidings of great joy, that shall be to
"'all the people: That is, that unto you
"'is borne this day a Saviour, Which is
"'Christ the Lord. And this shall be
"'a Signe unto you; you shall finde the
"'Childe swadled and layd in a Cratch.'
"And straight way there was with the
"Angell *a multitude of heavenly* Souldiers,
"*praysing* God, *and saying;* Glory be to
"God *in the high* Heaven, *and Peace on*
"Earth, *and towards men good will.* And
"it came to passe that when the Angels
"were gone away from thence into Heaven,
"that the Shepheards said one to another;

The Shepheards.

"'Let us goe then unto Bethlem, and see
"'this thing that is come to passe, which
"'the Lord hath shewed unto us;' so they
"came with haste, and found both Mary
"and Ioseph *with the* Babe *layd in the*
"Cratch. And when they had seene it,
"they publisht abroad the thing that was
"told them of that Childe."

 Here *three* things especially are remarkable:

Her Delivery.

First, their forwardnesse in believing:

Secondly, the speed they made to see what they had believed, and

Thirdly, to publish what they had seene.

That they quickly believed, appeares by the haste they made to see. They no sooner saw Him, but they found Him to be the *King* of *Israell* indeed, yet withall to be a *Shepheard*. They instantly discerne this to be the *Shepheard*, Who was to lay downe His Life for His Flocke. The *Prince* of all *Shepheards* Whose sheepe-fold is the world; the *Shepheard* that was to seperate the Goates from the Sheepe. They discover'd this to be the immaculate *Lambe* that was to take away the sinnes of the world. They disclos'd this *Lamb* to be the greatest *Lyon* of the *Tribe* of *Iudah*. Whom now they looke on in the Cratch, *Saint Iohn* shall hereafter behold on His Throne. These men, in whom there was no guile, as they could not deceive others, so they could not in this be deceived. They needed not suspect any fallacy, and therefore might safely relate this Divine Wonder to all they met.

Life of the Blessed Virgin:

The *second* witnesses of this Miracle are the *Wise-Men*. After GOD had laid open the Treasure of his Divine Secrets to Idiots, He shewes them also to the Wise. It seemes the *Earth*, at this time, was become the Booke of GODS greatest Mysteries, and *Heaven* the Index. In this they finde the Star of this *King* of the *Iewes*, which (having beene before the declarer of his Nativity) they now make their guide in their journey. The *Starre* performing this duty to its CREATOR, at length brings them to *Bethlem*, where they view Him in the Cratch, Whose Nativity before they had found in the *Heavens*. To Him they doe Homage, tender Adoration, and pay Tribute; and opening their Treasures, make him an Oblation of Gold, Incense, and Mirrhe. Whom before they had in vaine sought in the *Heavens*, they now finde on the *Earth;* and in the most sorded part of it, a Stable, full of severall stinkes; where He (to Whom none are worthy to be servants) had *two* dull Beasts for His Companions.

The Author " *Returne now you Sonnes of Wisedome to*

Her Delivery.

to the Wise-Men.

" *your owne home, by much more learned,*
" *by more than much more happy than when*
" *you set out.* Heaven *is now set open to*
" *you, which before your unbeliefe kept shut*
" *against you. If you be* Chaldeans *or*
" Persians, *or both, spreade through those*
" Nations *the fame of that which you have*
" *seene. Publish in all places this the*
" *greatest Mystery of Piety, which* God *is*
" *onely able to produce, onely Faith can ap-*
" *prehend. Of all Creatures to man onely*
" *belongs the gift of Reason, by the rule*
" *whereof he measures all things. But*
" *doe not you doe so, lest you fall not onely*
" *into an irreparable, but a damnable errour.*
" *Follow you the instruction of Faith, and*
" *where ere you come with a holy Pride,*
" *proclaime that* God *is manifested in the*
" *Flesh; justified in the* Spirit; *seene by*
" Angels; *reveal'd to* Shepheards; *found*
" *out, and ador'd, by you your selves; and*
" *hereafter to be assum'd, and to sit in*
" *Glory farre above those* Starres *you daily*
" *read. Goe, and give out that there is*
" *nothing greater in* Heaven, *than what*
" *you have found in a Stable. Yet ere you*

"depart, convince the ſtiffe-necked Iewes of
"their lofty, but groſſe errour, in diligently
"ſeeking to know GOD in that part wherein
"He will lye hid; and in taking no notice
"of Him in that part wherein He would
"be knowne: in looking for a SAVIOUR
"from* Heaven, who is already borne on
"Earth. Yet now I conſider their obſti-
"nacy better, I wiſh you to ſpare your here
"fruitleſſe adviſe: for. the eares of this
"wicked generation is ſtopped, their hearts
"obdurate, and they are as fully reſolved
"to goe on in their wickedneſſe, as you in
"your journey."

* The Iews whenever it lightneth, ſet open their windowes: for they hold their SAVIOUR ſhall come in Lightening. On this reade Buxdorfius.

Having proved His Nativity by theſe holy Teſtators; let us now enter ourſelves, and view this pretty one in his narrow lodging; lay ourſelves proſtrate before Him; worſhip Him; and recreate ourſelues with the lovely Object. And that our delight may be the greater, let us firſt behold Him, and His ſweeteſt *Mother* a part, and then both together. But let us here ſhut out the *Phariſees*, and barre them the ſight of this Heavenly INFANT, who urge the *Law*, and reject Him the Au-

THOR of it. Let us exclude the *Arrians*, who deny his Coequalitie with the FATHER; and the *Sabellians*, who confound the TRINITIE, of which He is distinctly One and hold that there is in It One *Essence*, and One *Person:* and the *Samosatenians*, who derogate from His Nature, and avouch the WORD (Which truly He is) to be no other then a vanishing Sound. Nor let us onely keepe out these, but the whole swarme also of *Atheists*, and *Hereticks*. Let the *Philosophers* too stay without, who not so impious, yet more ignorant, cannot dive to the bottome of this Mystery. But to all those who are honour'd in the Assumption and Profession of His glorious Name, a free Accesse is granted. Enter then you little Flock, you few whom His FATHER hath bestowed on Him; and see Him, Who when He gave the *Law* appeared in Fire, now He offers Grace involv'd in Hay. Yet in this dejected posture, in this course manner while He lay, He wanted not a whole Army of *Angelicall* Spirits that declar'd His Birth to Men; and they who had before chanted

His Praises as He sate in Glory, now sing His Goodnesse lying in the Cratch. Though He have a hoomely roofe over His Head, the *East* observes His Approach. Though the poverty of His Humanitie obscures His Deity, the *Starres* in *Heaven* make it known. Behold Him who came Humble to the humble, for the humble, and yet His Humility is above all sublimity. Reverently, and intentively, look on Him Who descended from *Heaven* to *Earth*; Who came to you, into you, Who is borne in the night, borne in the midst of Winter, and borne (after the wretched humane condition) naked, and none offer Him assistance. Swadling clothes are wanting; some ragges are found out; a Cradle is missing; a Manger is at hand.

The Author to the Reader.

" *Here He cryes to you, and holds up His*
" *pretty Hands to* Heaven, *which He cals*
" *to witnesse that He can humble Himselfe*
" *no lower. Can you view this humble,*
" *this mercifull spectacle, and not weepe*
" *your selues into marble? O speedily put*
" *on sackcloth! besprinckle your selues with*

> "*Ashes*; kneele downe in the duſt and
> "dung under the Manger, where your
> "Lord lyes; knock your ſelues on the
> "boſomes; fetch ſighs and grones from
> "the bottom of your hearts; repay Him
> "the teares He lent you; and by your
> "ſad geſture and deportment demonſtrate
> "how much you are bound to Him who
> "ſuffered for you even in His Birth."

Having ſeene the Sonne, now ſtedfaſtly place your eyes upon the *Mother*. Behold the unpolluted *Mayd* (a great part of the wonder) ſitting neare the Manger, being voyd of all luſt, chaſt in Soule and body, who doth now confeſſe that of which ſhe is not capable without a Miracle, to wit, that ſhe is a *Mother*; and with fixed eyes expreſſing now joy, now admiration, ſees her ſelfe wedded to *Heaven*. She beholds her ſelfe a *Mother* deliver'd of her *Parent*, a *Handmaid* of her *King* and *Maſter*. She, to her aſtoniſhment, finds that ſhe hath brought forth an Issue, more Mighty then *David*, more Ancient then *Adam*. And now ſhe feeles the tender, and ardent Affection of a *Mother*; but the old love ſhe hath borne her Virginity gives it an allay. Here the *Mother*, the *Midwife*, and the *Nurſe* are one, and the ſame; leſt any thing leſſe pure ſhould handle Him, then her who brought Him forth. And now ſhe nurſeth this Heavenly INFANT with her pure Milke, which flows from no mortall luſt, but from the Celeſtiall Grace. Her Breaſts, white as their owne milke, preſſed by her delicate fingers, as white as either, He ſoftly pats, and playes with. Sometimes He repaires to them for ſport; ſometimes for neceſſity; and He who feeds all things elſe, draws thence His nouriſhment. He caſteth up now one eye, now the other, and with a pleaſing looke gives her a ſweet ſmile; not unlike to that which *Zephirus* imprints on the cheeke of the *Roſe*. She returns Him another, and her infinite, but chaſte, affection ſhe divides betweene her SONNE, and her Virginity. And now her extaſie being a little over, ſhe cals to minde that ſhe hath often read her owne Story foretold by the *Prophets*, *That a* Virgin *ſhould bring forth a* SONNE.

"*Fly, O fly farre hence, you Monſters of*

Iſa. i. vii. 14.

The Author *to y*ᵉ *Feminine* Reader.

"women, who carry leprous Soules in pol-
"luted bodies; and have not one Vertue to
"rescue you from the Legion of your vices.
"Depart hence you who are slaves to Lust;
"whose fetters you have worne so long,
"that they have made a deepe impression
"in your mindes. You who have spent
"your time in the search after alluring
"dresses, and in wanton dalliance, shall
"have no entrance here. You who have
"received with delight one warme Mascu-
"line kisse, shall here be excluded. Nay, you
"who have had onely one unchaste thought,
"shall not here be admitted, without being
"prepared by a cleansing hearty Repentance.
"This is the lodging of Purity, into which
"nothing must come that is uncleane. But
"you whose chaste eyes have never sent out
"lustfull beames, nor received them in;
"whose Bosomes have beene of proofe against
"the fierce assaults, and batteries of Temp-
"tation; you are so farre from being for-
"bidden to come here, that you are ear-
"nestly invited hither. You who have
"lived spirituall Amourists, whose Spirits
"have triumphed over the flesh, on whose
"cheeks Solitude, Prayers, Fasts, and Aus-

"terity have left an amiable pale: You
"who ply your Sacred Arithmeticke, and
"have thoughts cold, and cleare as the
"Chriſtall beads you pray by: You who
"have vow'd Virginity mentall, and cor-
"porall, you ſhall not onely have ingreſſe
"here, but welcome. Approach with Com-
"fort, and kneele downe before the Grand
"White Immaculate Abbeſſe *of your ſnowy*
"Nunneries, *and preſent the* All-Saving
"Babe *in her Armes, with due Veneration.*
"*Never thinke more of the Fæcunditie of*
"*Wedlocke, ſince you ſee here that* God
"Himſelfe *is the* Fruit *of Virginity. You*
"*who have tyed your ſelves in holy Bonds,*
"*from which you wiſh never but by death*
"*to be freed, who have choſe, rather law-*
"*fully to yeeld to the rebellious deſires of*
"*the fleſh, than unlawfully to ſubdue them:*
"*You who in fidelity and ſimplicity of life,*
"*have ſtrictly imitated* Christ *and His*
"Spouſe: *You whoſe Fertility is bleſſed,*
"*not onely in preſerving and propagating*
"*the humane Race, but in augmenting alſo*
"*the number of the* Saints *in* Heaven, *to*
"*you a free and open acceſſe is given. You*

"*widdowed* Turtles, *who have loſt your*
"*Mates, and either have vowed never to*
"*match againe, or pray'd to* GOD *that when*
"*you doe, it may be to His Glory; you alſo*
"*ſhall have admittance.* Virgins, Wives,
"*and Widdowes, ioyne hands, and encircle*
"*this the moſt perfect paire that ever graced*
"*the earth: Behold to your aſtoniſhment,*
"*and alſo to your conſolation, a milde*
"*and gentle,* Maide, *in whom neither*
"*Childe-birth defaceth Virginity, nor Vir-*
"*ginity, Fruitfulneſſe. Feed your eyes with*
"*the ſight of her whoſe minde is a Para-*
"*dice without a Serpent, on whoſe lookes,*
"*words, and actions, Modeſty is a diligent*
"*attender. And now in Peace doe you depart*
"*too; but take this charitable Admonition*
"*along with you, that (in emulation of this*
"*your deareſt* Miſtreſſe) *you lay up all her*
"*graces and perfections in your hearts; and*
"*withall, continually meditate her patience,*
"*which contented it ſelfe with bad lodging,*
"*and worſe accommodation, the ſad remem-*
"*brance whereof hath made me ever ſince*
"*I read this paſſage, not to be very ſoli-*
"*citous where, or how I lye.*"

HER PURIFICATION.

AVING waited on her in her Delivery, we will now attend her to her Purification. This day (the celebration whereof is inſtituted by the *Church*) is called *Candlemaſſe*, as much as to ſay, the *Day of Lights*, on which (while Maſſe was ſinging) very many Tapours were burning in the *Church*. The Luſtration of houſes was yearely uſuall with the *Romans*, in the *Moneth* of *February*, from whence this cuſtome in the *Church* is derived. *Innocentius* thus propounds and ſolves the Queſtion. "*What is the reaſon*," ſaith he, "*that on this Holy Day we uſe ſo many* "*Lights in the* Church? *The cauſe of this* "*inſtitution is* two-fold. The firſt is, that

<small>Innocentius.
In ſerm. de Purif. B. Mar. Virg.</small>

Her Purification.

"*a* Heathenish *custome may be converted* "*into a* Christian *Right or Ordinance; and* "*that which was performed by superstitious* "*Idolators in honour of* Ceres *and* Proser- "pina, *may be turned into the praise and* "*Glory of the* Virgin Mary. *The* second "*is, that they who by Grace are purified,* "*by this Ceremony may be admonished to* "*imitate those prudent Virgins, who (as the* "Evangelicall *Parable testifieth) came not* "*without their Tapours lighted to the* "*Nuptials of* Christ *their Spouse.*" This day the *Church* used to pray, that as the visible Lights chased away the darknesse of the night; so the hearts of the Faithfull might be illuminated by the Invisible flames of the Holy Spirit, and (being cured of their blindnesse brought upon them by vice) might with pure and cleare eyes discerne those things which are pleasing to God, and necessary to their Salvation; and having pass'd through the sad, darke, and dismall accidents of this world, might at length arrive at *Heaven,* where they shall behold, and enjoy a Light everlasting. This day is not onely made Holy by the

Purification of the *Mother*, but by the Oblation alfo, and Prefentation of the SONNE, of Whom, as of the more worthy, we muft *firft* difcourfe.

It was truley a great abafing of the SONNE of GOD, (for which by the *Prophets* he was ftyled a Servant) Who being not a debtor to the Law, but the LORD of it, and the Onely FIRST-BORNE free from finne; yet endured, and underwent with other Children, both the *Iewifh* Circumcifion and Oblation, and at once publikely honour'd His FATHERS Houfe, and (to ufe the *Prophets* phrafe) fill'd it with Glory. There offer'd by the *Virgin* hands of His *Mother*, He was to His FATHER a moft pleafing Oblation, being the end of the Law, and all the antient Sacrifices. Neither was the longing of *Simeon* and *Anna* onely fatisfied with His Afpect; but the ardent wifhes alfo of many others, in whofe mindes the old fparke of Faith now burft out into new and bright flames, which did not onely illuminate their owne, but other bofomes alfo. Not a few, queftionleffe, at *Hierufalem*, markt this day

Her Purification.

with a white stone, and did celebrate it with joy and thankesgiving, in that the Light foretold by *Esay* then arose, and comforted all those to whom the shine and warmth of it extended. *Israel* had never seene her MESSIAS, till then when she had free leave to kisse, embrace, and dandle Him in her Armes; and therefore her joy must of necessity be more than ordinary. Yet some of her inhabitants were deafe, and could not heare the *Prophets* proclaime His comming; others were blinde, and could not discerne Him being come, nor were sensible at all of the Honour they received in the venerable presence of Him, and His incomparable *Mother*.

I now come to our sweetest *Lady*, the time of whose Lying-in being expired, she sets forward to the *Temple*. I have reade some who poetically set downe her going thither, and compare her to *Aurora*, whom the *Poets* describe, sitting in a golden Chariot drawn by a *Pegasus*, her yellow haire spred over her milky shoulders, with a torch in her hand enlightning this inferiour world. For my owne part (though of all humane ſtudies I am moſt taken with Poeſy) yet both by Nature and Grace I abhorre to write of things Divine in the ſtile of the ſtage. But this Religion and Modeſty will licenſe me to averre, That when ſhe went to be Purified, ſhe was in all things the very figure and reſemblance of Sanctity it ſelfe. No doubt but ſhe was accompanied with a beavy of *Shee-Saints*, of which ſhe was the *Chorus*. Neither was *Ioſeph* abſent; who as before he had beene a guardian of her, and her INFANT in her Delivery, when he was not capable of the Miracle; ſo now he is altogether incapable of his owne Felicity, in attending his faireſt *Mate*, and deareſt MASTER to the Holy *Temple*. And who doubts but this Bleſſed *One* joy'd more in this Iourney than *Ioſeph*, or any other. *Saint Iohn* and *Saint Luke* teſtifie that it was a Religious Cuſtome amongſt the very *Heathen* from remote places to come to *Hieruſalem*; and in the *Temple* thereof to performe their devotions. Doe you thinke this pious *Maide* can be out-ſtripped in the performance of a Holy Duty by the *Gentiles*?

Iohn 12.
Acts ii. 8.

Can you imagine she could neglect, and loose the occasion of time, and place offered her, to commend to her MAKER, in her best words, the Vowes and Prayers of her prepared Heart? She came to *Hierusalem* (for certainly she dwelt not there) with farre greater speed and joy, questionlesse, than to her *Cousins* House; this being a businesse that much more concern'd her, in that she was by more and stronger tyes bound to serve GOD than *Elizabeth*.

And here by the way we must not omit her Humility, and Charity. Of the *first* whereof we have a cleere demonstration in this, That what other women did out of feare of the Law, she was perswaded by a perfect Faith, and an humble Obedience to performe. For that her Purification was necessary, I beleeve no man will affirme, unlesse in this sense, That the Rites and Ceremonies imposed on the purified by *Moses*, were with decency to be observed by her, who had borne Him that came to fulfill, not to destroy the Law. She could not be maculated in conceiving, because she knew no man; nor in bearing, by

Her Humility.

reason it was without a man. Why should she be solicitous to redeeme her SONNE, Who was Himselfe the REDEEMER of the world? This was assuredly an Act produced by her Humility; as was also her refusing the company of the rich, and her associating the poore and needy, though most impure, and abject.

Her Charity.

And she her selfe was so poor, that she had not wherewithall to buy a *Lambe*, whereof to make oblation. Whereof the Rich hide and hourd up their wealth, she drawes forth the* Treasure brought her by the *Wise Men*, and with alacrity distributes it amongst those whose wants required it: yet was part of the present gold, which upon charitable uses surely was consumed; for her Frugality, and Temperancy were such, that in so short a time she could not possibly have spent the value of it. But these Perfections are not to be wondred at in her, who being a *Doctresse*, scorn'd not to be a *Disciple*; and strongly to endeavour the attaining even to those Vertues which by Nature were innate, and by Grace engrafted in her. Ravisht in Soule with

* *This is the observation of* Dammianus, Dammasce *& many more.*

these her Excellencies, me thinkes I see her Majestically pacing on to the *Temple*, and heare her thus speake to those who accompanied and met her on the way.

   " *My deare Friends, Sisters, and fellow* "*Servants, I have ever desir'd and endea-* "*vour'd, (as neare as Humane frailtie* "*will give me leave) to imitate my sweetest* "SONNE, *whose profound Humility and* "*perfect Obedience can never sufficiently* "*be extolled. Full well He knew Humility* "*to make the* first *step to Eternall Life;* "*Obedience the* second; *the former of which* "*to teach all men He descended from* Hea- "ven, *the latter to demonstrate, He became* "*obedient to His* FATHER, *even to the* "*suffering of the cursed death of the Crosse.* "*Would you see me a Proficient in both* "*these supernaturall Vertues? Behold me* "*who am unpolluted, (as not having con-* "*ceived by humane meanes) going like one* "*vitious, and impure to be purified. I who* "*am free from the observation of the* Mo- "saicall Lawes *and* Ceremonies, *have sub-* "*jected my selfe to them. I who am voyd* "*of all wilfull sinne, willingly goe amongst*

S. Mary *to her* Friends.

"other sinfull and uncleane women, that I
"may be to all an Example of Charity
"and Humility, to none a President of
"ruine. I thought it not enough that my
"fruitfull Virginity had produced Salva-
"tion to the world, unlesse by Example
"also I taught how this Grace (applicable
"to all, applied but to a few) by you also
"might be obtained. This is my way to
"the attainement of Celestiall Glory; and
"let it be yours to purchase your selves
"Eternall Salvation. Doe thus, live thus,
"that you may shine holy Tapers in GODS
"Militant Church, and glorious Stars in
"His Triumphant."

She, with her devout traine, being come into the *Temple* offer'd her gift to the *Priest*, and received a Propheticke Benediction from *Symeon*. Whether this old Man were a *Priest*, or a *Layman*, I will not here dispute; certainly he was a Man blessed above all the *Patriarchs* and *Prophets*, in that he saw GOD face to Face; and may be styled the most profound of all *Divines*, who (being the last just man of the Law, the first of Grace, a *Iew*, by

<small>Timoth. presb. Hierosol. in orat. de Propheta Simeone.</small>

Her Purification.

Religion, in Thankſgiving a *Chriſtian*) comprehended ſo many Myſteries, in ſo few words. This Holy Man (the *Scribes* and *Phariſees* dreaming on no ſuch matter) had long ſince ſeene his SAVIOUR comming; Whom he no ſooner ſaw borne into the *Temple* by His *Mother* (who then reſembled Modeſty ſupporting Sanctity) but he ſnatcht this prettie BABE out of her armes into his owne; and not able to containe his joy, in a Divine Rapture, Swanne-like, (his death being then at hand) ſung this his ſweeteſt Ditty. " 'LORD, *now* [S. Symeon.]
" ' *letteſt thou thy Servant depart in Peace:*
" ' *for mine eyes have ſeene Thy Salvation,*
" ' *Which Thou haſt prepared before the*
" ' *face of all* Nations; *a Light to lighten*
" ' *the* Gentiles, *and to the glory of Thy peo-*
" ' *ple* Iſrael.' And he bleſſed them, and ſaid
" unto Mary his mother, ' Behold this
" ' CHILDE *is appointed for the fall and*
" ' *riſing againe of many in* Iſrael, *and for*
" ' *a ſigne which ſhall be ſpoken againſt, yea*
" ' *and a ſword ſhall paſſe through thy Soule,*
" ' *that the thoughts of many hearts may be*
" ' *opened.*' And Anna a Propheteſſe con- [S. Anna.]

"fessed the same to all those who looked for
"the Redemption of Israel."

If the viewing and embracing of CHRIST so dilated the Spirits of the old Mans heart, and made him so sensible of this his great felicitie, that he would expect here no greater, but desired rather a dissolution then the fruition of any thing else on earth, What may we judge her content to be, who conceiv'd, bore, brought forth, and brought Him up? Whose affectionate looks, kisses, and embraces He had by day; the two later of which the night it selfe could not barre Him of. Her greatest detractors surely, cannot imagine her so stupid as not to be apprehensive of the Delight, the Comfort, the Happinesse, the Honour His Presence did impart; nor so unthankfull as not to acknowledge, and to her power, expresse her gratitude. Certainly her Soule was in a Heavenly Trance, when she contemplated the Grace and felicity she had in GODS Owne House; and before an Assembly of his elected People, to acknowledge her gratitude for the inestimable benefits he had vouchsafed her, but especially for this, That, in His Glorious Eyes, she seem'd worthy (though in her selfe undeserving) in her owne name, and that of His chosen, to present Him with such a Sacrifice, such a Gift as exceedingly surpassed in excellency, all Hosts, Sacrifices, and Sacraments whatsoever, being indeed, their onely scope and end. *Anna*, the Mother of *Samuel* is praised for her diligence in Prayer, the fruit whereof she reaped in her dispair'd of Fertility. And of our admired *Virgin*, we reade that she carefully frequented the *Temple*, of which (being wise) she knew the institution, and (being pious) the custome, which she most religiously observed. Wherefore this day of her *Purification*, and at all times else, without all peradventure, she much excelled *Anna*, and her whole sexe in the fervency of her Orisons, in the ardency of her Love, in Purity, and Sublimity of minde, in Holinesse of life, and Divine Contemplation. We may boldly conclude, that she pour'd out her prayers here, in greater abundance than she did in *Zacharies* House, where she could not suppresse the flame of her Zeale from breaking out into the praise of GOD her SAVIOUR, in Whom she rejoyced. To this effect, happily, here she pray'd.

S. Mary's Prayer.

"*O eternall and Gracious* GOD! *I am below other women in merit, but above them all indebted to Thy Supreme Maiesty, for making me the* Tabernacle *of Thy Onely* SONNE, *the* Temple *of Thy* SPIRIT, *and for this speciall Honour done mee in the Temple of Thy Service, the congregation whereof makes me the onely point wherein the lines of their Affection, and Admiration doe meete. If women be respected for their fertillity, needs must I be in great esteeme with all men, who (by Thy eternall Predestination, and Fatherly Providence) have brought forth Thy Onely* SONNE, *their* REDEEMER. *With a bowed heart, and bended knees I acknowledge that Thou hast faithfully, and mercifully fulfilled all those Thy favourable promises, made me by Thy* Angell *Gabriel, my Cousin Elizabeth, and Thy holy* Prophets. *Thou who can'st neither deceive, nor be deceived, hast made me*

Her Purification.

"(*the Vertue of thy* Spirit *operating*) *a*
"Mother, *my Virginall integrity still pre-*
"*served.* That *long long'd for* Emanuel,
"(*than Whom nothing greater, or better*
"*could be given by Thee, or taken by me*)
"*I have at length produc'd to save all*
"*those that beleeve in Him.* This *mag-*
"*nificent, immense, inexhaustible, unva-*
"*luable Treasure, this beloved* Sonne *of*
"*Thine in Whom thou art well pleased;*
"*this* Saint *of* Saints, *by Whom all things*
"*in Heaven and Earth, are re-establisht,*
"*this* Saviour *of the world, I here present*
"*to Thee, as a Gift most acceptable in Thy*
"*Sight.* He *Whom all* Nations, *and the*
"Fathers *themselves have so much thirsted*
"*to see:* The Angell *of the New Testa-*
"*ment, the* Seed *of* Abraham, *the* Sonne
"*of* David, *the* King *of* Israel, *in Whom*
"*all generations are blessed, the* Lord *of*
"*the Temple, is here come to illustrate His*
"*Owne House.* O *mercifull* Father!
"*open the eyes of the dimme sighted Is-*
"*raelites, that they may see the glorious*
"*Light that now shines on them, and not*
"*onely acknowledge, but worship their*

"Messias, *and imbrace Him in their
hearts, as I doe in mine armes. Neither
let the Rayes of this new borne* Starre
*reflect onely on them, but on all those also,
who sit in darknesse, and the shadow of
death, that to them It may restore life
and lustre. So shall they acknowledge
Thee, and Him Whom Thou hast sent,*
Christ Iesus, *and be made Spirituall
Dwellings for Thee to reside in, there to
receive due thankes and praise, for ever,
and ever.*"

HER MOTHERLY CARE, TOGETHER WITH HER CONJUGAL FAITH AND OBEDIENCE.

ETWEENE her Purification, and Passion of her SONNE, she is not often mentioned in *Holy Writ*, but when she is, it is still to her Praise and Honour: As when her care for the Poor made her petition CHRIST for Wine to revive, and refresh their drooping, fainting Spirits; And when she said to Him, "*Why have You us'd us thus? Your Father and I have beene to seeke You.*" Whence all women may learne Humility, motherly Care, and conjugall Faith. She who was without blemish, as, as being GODS Owne *Mother*, whose chaste bosome no carnall

S. Mary.

thought had ever entred; who lookt on all men with the fame Innocency and Simplicity with which fhe beheld Statues; deigned to call a poor, ruftical, labouring man, Hufband; from whofe deare company, no flight, terrour, travaile, nor paines could feparate her. But what the *Scripture* omitteth, muft be fupplied by our charitable Imagination, which cannot but conceive all thofe her Actions buried in filence, to have beene of the fame pure thred with the reft of her life. The truth of which we finde confirm'd, in her perfeverance in Goodneffe, even to her Sonnes end, and her owne.

contristavi te · responda · mihi ·

HER DEMEANOUR AT HER SONNES DEATH, AND HER PASSIVE FORTITUDE AND PATIENCE.

T His death wee reade fhe was present, "*and there stood (saith the* Evangelift) *by the Croffe of* Christ *His* Mother *and her Sifter* Mary Cleophœ *and* Mary Magdalen. *When therefore* Iesus *saw His* Mother, *and His beloved* Disciple *standing by, He said to His* Mother, *'* Woman, *behold thy* Son,' *and He said to His* Disciple, *'* Behold thy Mother,' *and from that time he tooke her for his.*" His pardoning of the *Thiefe*, is not a greater argument of His Mercy; than His taking care for His *Mother*, was of His Piety.

S. John xix. 25.

He gives Temperancy the cuſtody of Chaſtity, and commends theſe to each other who were reſolved to live and dye Virgins. *Saint Bernard* ſayes theſe words of CHRIST to his *Mother*, included much bitterneſſe; for they put her in minde that ſhe was to make a dammageable exchange of CHRIST for *Iohn;* of the *Servant* for His LORD; of the *Diſciple* for his MASTER; of the SONNE of GOD, for the ſonne of *Zebedæus.* And this was the reaſon (if we give beliefe to *Mantuan*) that He called her *Woman*, not *Mother*, leſt the very ſound of that deare word ſhould make her more ſenſible of His approaching loſſe, and force her into an immoderate griefe. But ſorrow was no Noveltie to her; for that ſaying of CHRIST, " *In this world, you ſhall have afflic̄tion,*" was in her verified, whoſe life contained more miſeries than minuts, which ſhe patiently underwent; knowing that the more diſtreſſed ſhe was here, the more bleſſed ſhe ſhould be hereafter. And if we ſhall adde the light of Reaſon to the Evangelicall Truth, we ſhall ſoone perceive that a fatall sadnesse haunted her from the Birth of her onely SONNE to His Buriall. When she was great with Him, and readie to lye downe, the inhumanity of the *Bethlemites* was such, that they confined her, and the LORD of all things to a Stable; and would not supply her with as much as Linnen, a Mantle, and other necessaries wherewithall she might defend her selfe, and her sweet BABE from the moysture of the night, the sharpenesse of the winter, and other intollerable inconveniences. When her CHILDE was *eight daies* old, she saw Him loose Bloud in His Circumcision, which her divining Soule misgave her, to be a Type of the deare Remainder He was to shed. Then againe her Minde was infinitely vexed for the butchery of those guiltlesse Children, which were murthered for the sake of her owne Innocent INFANT; of the sorrow and miserie of whose Mothers, her tender compassionating Heart was a most competent Iudge. From this bloudy Massacre to save her SAVIOUR, she was constrained (without taking leave of her friends, or disposing of what was hers) to take her Flight with Him, & through danger,* darknesse, and horrour, to make her way into *Egypt.* When He was *twelve yeeres* old, she lost Him, an accident more grievous than any of the former; for heretofore, her study had been, to preserve What she had; now, her care was, to finde What she had not. What an Agony her Soule suffer'd at the lamentable tydings of the beheading of her Sonnes *Forerunner*, I leave to the consideration of all thankeful Soules; for she could not without being stayned with ingratitude, but mourne for his absence, and violent departure out of the world, who had received so much joy at her presence before he came into it. But above all these, the unequall'd Treacherie of *Iudas*, who deliver'd this Lambe of God, as a prey to these Wolves; the infidelity of His other *Disciples*; the malignity of His *Iudges*; the cruelty of His *Executioners*, conspir'd to make her miserable. Nor is it unlikely that she bewailed the ingratitude, the obstinacy, and impiety of her *Nation*, who revil'd Him That blessed them, and tortur'd

* Vernulæus *saies that those who flye from danger, travaile most by night; and therefore it is likely our* Blessed Lady *did so.*

Demeanour at Her Sonnes *Death.*

Him Who came to save them. With what amazement, and sadnesse was her Heart surprised think ye, when the newes came of her SONNES being apprehended? But when she saw Him forsaken by His Friends; bound by His enemies; accused before the *High Priests*; derided by *Herod*; despis'd by the *People*; scourg'd, and tortur'd by the command of *Pilate*; His Body trembling, torne, and pierced; besmear'd with His Owne Bloud; and hung between *two Theeves*; then, and never till then did the Sword foretold by *Simeon*, passe through her Soule. *Luther* saies this Prophecy of *Simeon* was spoken to her, not to *Ioseph*; for on her alone the whole weight of sorrow was to be laid. True it is, that many differ about the interpretation of this Sword. To cleare all doubts, we must take notice that the *Holy Scriptures* mention *foure* sorts of Swords. [Luther.]

The *first* is a Corporall, or materiall Sword; and of this CHRIST speakes to Peter, "*All that use the Sword, shall perish* "*with the Sword.*" [The Corporal Sword. S. Matt. xxv. 52.]

The *second*, is a spiritual Sword, of [The Spiritual Sword.]

which *Saint Paul* makes mention, when he faies, "*Receive the Sword of the* SPIRIT, "*which is the* WORD *of* GOD." <small>Eph. vi. 17.</small>

The *third*, is a Sword of Scandall, or Ambiguity, with which the *Apoſtles* themſelves were ſtrucken, when they forſooke their MASTER. <small>The Sword of Scandall.</small>

The *fourth*, is the Sword of Griefe, or Tribulation. With this the *Prophet David* averres the Soule of *Ioſeph* to have beene pierc'd when his death was plotted firſt by his trecherous Brothers, next by his incontinent Miſtreſſe. <small>The Sword of Griefe. Pſal. xxxiii. Pſal. cv. Gen. xxxvii.</small>

That this Sword whereof *Simeon* Prophecied, could be no materiall one, is evident; in that we read not of any violent death ſhe ſuffered. That it could not be the Sword of the SPIRIT, is manifeſt; for the *Word* of GOD was her daily delitious food at the ſame time when *Simeon* made this Prophecy. *Origen* indeed will have it to be the ſword of Ambiguity or Infidelity: which erroneous opinion of his, is refuted by many great *Fathers* of the Antient *Church*, and by *Franciſcus Lambertus*, an accute *Proteſ-* <small>In expoſit. Evang. Lucæ cap. 2.</small>

tant *Doctor* of the Moderne, in these words: "*Those, (saith he,) who will have this to be the Sword of Infidelity, are not to be hearkened to; for (besides that they can produce no proofe of this their opinion) it is contradictory to the Text, most rash, and most untrue. How can it be that the Sword of Infidelity should penetrate the brest of* Gods *Sacred* Mother, *into which, infidelity never made the least impression? From the beginning her Faith was most firme and intire. Let therefore those blasphemies, and wicked slanders of carnall men be put to silence. I will attribute nothing to the* Blessed Virgin, *but what I reade in the* Holy Writ, *where she is pronounced* Blessed, *because shee beleev'd. We have many testimonies of her Faith; but of her Infidelity not one word is extant in the Sacred* Scriptures."

Yet this profane assertion is not a whit strange, or to be marvelled at in *Origen*, who held that Christ dyed for the *Angels*, and the *Starres*; and whose Soule was, indeed, no other than a *Mynt of Heresies*. *Melancton* affirmes, that her sorrow was

Melan. in cap. 27. Matth.

much aſſwaged by her Faith, which aſſured her of His Reſurrection. She knew ſhe had borne the MESSIAS, whoſe Bloud was to waſh away the ſinnes of the world. Wherefore ſhe might well be amaz'd, diſtruſtfull ſhe could not be at all. The HOLY SPIRIT certified her this was not a deſtroying Death, but a Triumphing. Her Faith, the oftener it was tryed in the Furnace of affliction, the brighter ſtill it ſhewed. She ſtood with the affection of a *Mother*, the paſſion of a woman, but with the conſtancy and fortitude of a man, in beholding her owne Bloud ſpilt, her owne Fleſh rent, and mangled before her face. With an unſhaken Confidence, and a true internall Valour, ſhe beheld His Body naked, and ſcourg'd; His Hands and Feet nailed to the Croſſe: yet ſometimes the ſtrings of her relenting, mournefull heart were ready to cracke with the very thought of His cruell tortures, and afflictions; but as often againe they were ſtrengthened, and comforted with a full aſſurance that He ſhould overcome them all, and Death it ſelfe. She ſtood here (her SONNE onely excepted) the prime Patterne of a follid Faith, and conftant Patience, to all pofteritie; in that neither the feare of Tribulation, of Perfecution, of the Wracke, of the Scourge, or Death it felfe, could divide her from her CHRIST. She committed not that errour moft incident to women, many of which gentle fexe perifh in the midft of their Lamentations, and will neither admit of Counfell, nor Comfort. She did not teare her haire; fcratch her face; batter her bofome; feeke to ftifle her felfe ; or gave any other defperate figne of a ragefull Sorrow ; nor did fhe curfe her enemies, or make imprecations for Vengeance, or fo much as murmur againft them: but attended the fad Event with the fame calmeneffe of Minde with which this meeke LAMBE did His End. Her carriage was beyond the Levell of Cenfure; and in all things fuitable to the modefty and gravity of fuch a *Matron*. She fear'd not at all the fury of the *Iewifh Souldiers*, that environ'd her, but ftood fecure, and fac'd Danger. Though fhe was an eye witneffe of His Paffion, and saw His Limbs diftended, and wrack'd; yet did not the evils fhe faw, wound her fo deep as thofe fhe heard. The *Roman* Fencers ufed to have Wards, or Covers to fave their Eares; fhe had greater need of fuch to barre the entrance of blafphemies able to provoke GOD (if His Mercies were not above all His Workes) utterly to deface *Nature*, and reduce the world to its *firft* Chaos. She heard Him call'd a Drunkard, a Blafphemer, a Breaker of the Sabboth, a Lover of Publicans and Sinners, nay a very Divell, Who was her, and GODS Onely Delight. Yet did not all thefe killing objects, thefe impious flanders, drive her into the mercileffe gripes of Defpaire; for fhe was confident that the TWO PERSONS of the TRINITY would not forfake the THIRD. *Melancton* commending this difmal Story to our fad and ferious contemplation, advifeth us; That when Tribulations and Death it felfe come upon us, we fhould imitate this *Holy Virgin*, who mixed a Heart killing forrow for His death with a joy-full affurance of His Refurrection. "Con-

_{Melan. in loco prædic.}

Demeanour at Her Sonnes Death.

"*sider (saith he) what a Conflict the Faith of* Mary *had. There was in her an extreme Griefe, linked with Faith and Hope. Let us in our death thus comfort our selves, and harbour the same thoughts with* Mary, *still fixing on* God *the eyes of our Faith.*" And verily we must beleeve, that no small measure of Beliefe was required to temper and asswage so great a* sorrow. If we conceive that she was so without bowels, as not to grieve for the Death and Passion of her dearest, and only Sonne: we must withall beleeve with the *Maniches*, that He had a phantasticke Body, not made of his *Mothers* Flesh. No doubt, when (after man had left, and betray'd Him) she heard Him cry out that God Himselfe had forsaken Him also, her teares, her sighes, her groanes, her countenance, her very posture, her dolefull voyce, all united their forces to expresse the greatnesse of her sorrow. Listen and you shall heare her thus lament.

* Sophronius. ser. de Assump. Beatæ Virg. *maintains that she suffered more than all the Martyrs, in that the passion of the Minde is greater than that of the body; and shee in Soule felt most, because her love to Him was above all others.*

HER LAMENTATION.

<small>Her Lamentation is also expressed by S. Bernard, Serm. qui incipit, Signum magnum.</small>

MY dearest SONNE, that Thou
"Who healest others, shouldst
"Thy Selfe be wounded! That
"Thou Who freest others,
"shouldst Thy Selfe be bound! That Thou
"Who art the FOUNTAINE of Life, and
"CREATOR of the waters, shouldst Thy
"Selfe be thirsty! That Thou Who
"cloathest all things, shouldest Thy Selfe
"stand naked! O my dearest MASTER, how
"hast Thou trespassed against this obdurate
"Nation! that it should so thirst after
"Thy pretious Bloud? Thou wouldest
"have cover'd them under the wings of
"Thy gratious Providence, as a Henne
"doth her Chickens, but they chose rather
"to perish, than to come thither for shelter.

LAMENTATION.

"MY dearest SONNE, that Thou
"Who healest others, shouldst
"Thy Selfe be wounded! That
"Thou Who freest others,
"shouldst Thy Selfe be bound! That Thou
"Who art the FOUNTAINE of Life, and
"gavest the waters, shouldst Thy
"Selfe be dry! That Thou Who
"coverest all things, shouldest Thy Selfe
"stand naked!! O my dearest MASTER, how
"hast Thou trespassed against this obdurate
"Nation! that it should so thirst after
"Thy pretious Bloud? Thou wouldest
"have cover'd men under the wings of
"Thy gratious Providence, as a Henne
"doth her Chickens, but they chose rather
"to perish, than to come thither for shelter.

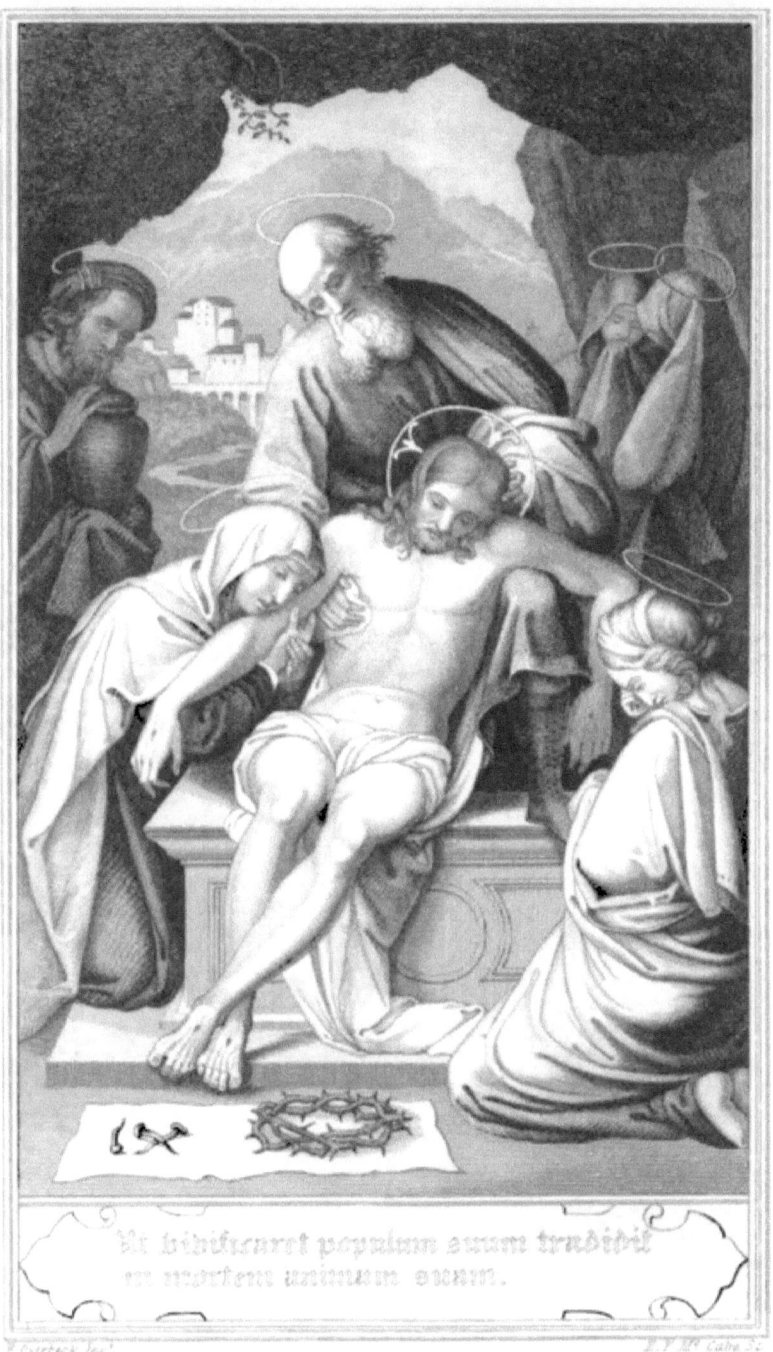

"*With them the dead are more sensible of*
"*Thy Passion, than the living; and their*
"*devouring Sepulchers more mercifull then*
"*they themselves.* O my SONNE, my
"SONNE, *that I should see Thee suffer,*
"*and not be able to succour Thee! O that*
"*I were an* Oblation *as spotlesse, and as*
"*gratious in Thy* FATHERS *Sight, as*
"*Thou Thy Selfe; that all Thy afflic-*
"*tions, all Thy torments might be mine.*
"*Were my power correspondent to my will,*
"*I would rescue Thee from Legions of*
"*Thy enemies. But alas I am a weake*
"Woman; *and all my strength lyes in my*
"*tongue, which will onely serve mee to de-*
"*plore Thy losse, and that I truely doe from*
"*the very bottome of my heart.*"

Thus, or to this purpose, questionlesse she bewail'd Him Dying; but when she once beheld Him Dead (Love and Beauty being banisht that Face), and saw withall their malitious cruelty survive Him; when she view'd His very Carkasse pierc't, and Water together with Bloud flowing thence; when she had leisure to imbrace His Dead Body, to number His Wounds, to kisse them, and to essay with the holy Water of her eyes to wash away His Stripes: she then was so wholly oppressed with anguish of Soule, that she ardently, at that instant desired her Soule, if possibly, might transmigrate out of her living body, into His dead one. True it is, that many affirme she felt not those torments which other women endure in Child-birth, who are liable to the malediction laid upon *Eve*: but if at His Comming into the world, she was not sensible of any paine at all, certainely at His Going out, the griefes of all women contracted into one, equals not hers alone. And assuredly, her sorrow was much increased when she saw *Mary Magdalen*, and the other women so vehemently to grieve, whom His Death not so nearly concern'd as it did her; nor were they so able as she to judge of His Value. Then questionlesse in this, or the like phrase she renewed, and redoubled her Complaints:

S. Mary's Lamentation.

"*O my sweetest* Sonne! *I bewaile
" mine owne, and the wretched condition
" of all those, whose Soules Thou hast*

"feasted so many yeares with Thy mel-
"lifluous Language. My griefe is an-
"swerable to my affection. If Samuel la-
"mented the death of a reprobate King;
"if David wept over wicked Absolon
"with this exclamation, 'Absolon, my
"'Sonne, O my Sonne Absolon;' can my
"tears be too prodigally powr'd upon Thee,
"who art SONNE to me, and RIGHTEOUS-
"NESSE It Selfe? Who shall forbid, or hin-
"der me from crying out, 'IESUS, my sweet
"SONNE, O my sweet SONNE IESUS?'
"If Thou didst weep over Ierusalem, as
"lamenting her destruction then at hand,
"shall I not bewaile Thy neere approach-
"ing End? Thou didst then compassionate
"the future ruine of those very stones,
"which now with a silent gratitude seeme
"to condole, and weepe for Thee. When
"Thou cam'st to the Tombe of Lazarus,
"Thou wert so farre from reprehending
"the teares of others, that Thou wepst Thy
"Selfe for company. Thy Owne Example
"then warrants the justnesse of my griefe;
"for when Thou wert living, the small
"paine Thou felt'st in the sleeping of Thy

"Foot was, and ought to be more to mee,
"than the eternall sleepe of Lazarus could
"be to Thee. And as Thy Teares for him
"were tokens of Thy Humane Nature, not
"signes of Thy Diffidence (in that Thou
"knew'st he would forthwith arise); so
"are mine for Thee, witnesses of my
"wretched estate, not of my distrust, who
"am assured of Thy speedy Resurrection.
"Nor doe I onely grieve my owne griefe;
"for as for mans sake, I rejoyce in Thy
"FATHERS Grace, who delivers Thee to
"Death, and in Thy Charity who dost
"suffer it: So likewise, in mans behalfe,
"I am griev'd that he should be the cursed
"cause of those Thy extreme Torments:
"For as not to joy in the benefits Thy
"Death hath brought with it, would
"argue his ingratitude; so not to condole
"for the Tortures that attend it, would
"demonstrate his cruelty. And here I
"faithfully promise Thee, that both I,
"while life, and Thy Church, while the
"world, doth last, shall yearely spend this
"dolefull* time of Thy Tragicall Expira-
"tion in prayer, fasting, severity, of dis-

*S. Bernard cals this Hebdoma-

"cipline, maceration of the flesh, and con-"trition of the Spirit, as becomes *Thy* "**mournful** Mother, *and Thy* gratefull "Spouse *to doe.*"

Thus condoling, thus bemoaning hers, and the generall losse, she attended His Herse to the Sepulchre provided by *Ioseph*, where never man was laid before; for it was not fit that Incorruptibility should succeed corruption in the same lodging. This Fragrant FLOWER was no sooner set in the ground, but she sent many a deare drop after it to fasten it at the root; for she knew within *three dayes* It should spring up againe, not to grow in the earth, but to be translated into *Heaven*, there for ever to flourish, and perfume the Celestiall Habitation. Nor were her eyes, saith *Damascen*, closed with his Monument, but watched themselves almost blinde with a greedy expectation to see the Temple of His Body built up againe, which *three dayes* since was destroyed. After many a longing looke she espied the Tombe to open, and her onely Joy to issue forth, whom full well she knew by

dam pœnosam, the Weeke of Pennance; and the high Dutch, Die Martyr Wocken, *the* Martyrs *Weeke.*

Damascen.

the Countenance and Figure of His Humanity, but farre better by the cleere proofes of His GODHEAD; for the Graves delivered up their dead, many of which appear'd to their friends in the *Holy City.* Some, and those of great authority in the *Church* affirme, that after His Resurrection, she of all others saw Him *first;* and wheras the *Scripture* seemeth to inferre that *Mary Magdalen first* beheld Him, they thus expound it; That the *Evangelists* would not make His *Mother* the *first Witnesse* of His Resurrection (though indeed she was) knowing that her testimony by the *Iewes* would be more suspected than that of *Mary Magdalen.* I dare not positively conclude any thing herein, but I may safely maintaine that this her delight for His Resurrection, counterpois'd her griefe conceived for His Death. In her was now made good that of the *Psalmist*; *According to the multitude of the griefes of my heart, Thy Comforts have rejoyced my Soule*, and that of her SONNE; *Blessed are they that mourne, for they shall bee comforted.*

S. Matt. v. 4.

And who makes queſtion but that ſhe who with ſuch unutterable pleaſure diſcover'd His Reſurrection faithfully, and cloſely waited on Him, till His Aſcention? She who was as inſeparable to Him as His Shadow, without doubt, was on the *Mount* Olivet*, with other of the Faithfull, when in the ſight of them all He Aſcended. She heard, doubtleſſe, His laſt Words; received His laſt Benediction; and her ſight waited on Him, till the clowds imbrac't Him, which it in vaine eſſay'd to penetrate. What Soule not it ſelfe tranſported with the view of a Heavenly Object, can ſuppoſe, much leſſe expreſſe what her contentment was, when ſhe ſaw her owne Fleſh flye above the reach of envie, into the Armes of Glory? When ſhe beheld this HIGH PRIEST, (His Sacrifice ended, and GOD fully appeas'd) enter *Heaven* there to ſit on the Right Hand of His FATHER, and to be the unceſſant and eternall MEDIATOUR betwixt Him and man? With bended knees, erected hands, and eyes, ſhe worſhips Him aſcending, and when her ſight

* Epiphanius contra hæreſ. & libel. Ætij.

failes, her Adoration continues. Her Zeale passeth all the orbes betweene Him and her, with greater facility, and subtility then the Lightning shooteth through the Ayre. Great is the Vigour and Force of the Spirit, when all things else set apart, it is wholly intentive on the Meditation of its CREATOUR. When by contemplation, it is separated from the body, it thinkes onely on Him, lives onely to Him, and is (as it were drown'd) in an inundation of His Love. When it hath extinguisht the scorching lawlesse desires of the flesh, and kindled the holy ones of the SPIRIT; the body rebels no longer, but becomes obedient to it in all things. When it hath once fixed its eyes on this Beloved Object, it never removeth them thence. When it is once illuminated with the beames of the HOLY GHOST, it is presently turn'd into all Eye, all Spirit, all Light; no otherwise than those things the fire once layes hold on, are turn'd into fire it selfe. Of those who live in Wedlocke, it is said that they are two in one flesh; and why may it not be said of

Her Lamentation.

CHRIST and the Soule wedded to Him, that they are two in One SPIRIT? And if ever it might be reported of any, furely of this *Holy Virgin*, who (though fhe was devided from her REDEEMER in Body) yet in Soule fhe was united to Him. When her eyes were growne dimme with her fo long dwelling on that part of *Heaven* where they left, and loft Him, fhe caft them downe on the earth, the poverty whereof fhe commiferated, in that it was deprived of this one IEWELL, in value above all it had left. And now fhe returnes into the *Holy City*, not difconfolate, and dejected as other women are when they lofe their onely childe; but with a cheerfull look for her SONS Victory, Who had triumphed not onely over the *Iew*, but Death and Hell it felfe. She made her will lacky GODS; and though fhe defired to be diffolved, and be with CHRIST, yet fince it was His beft Pleafure fhe fhould continue longer here below, fhe readily affented, refolving by her example on earth, to furnifh *Heaven* with *Saints*. *Dammianus* fayes, that after her

Dammianus.

SONNES Deceafe, fhe remained *ten daies* in Prayer and Fafting, expecting with a fervent longing, the promifed comming of the SPIRIT. *Saint Luke* witneffeth, that *fixe fcore* men and women were affembled in one rome, and joyned in hearty Prayer, of the which, *Mary*, the *Mother* of IESUS, was *one*. And as He names her laft, fo her wonted Humility perfwades me, that fhe had the laft, and* loweft place, and fate beneath the other finfull women of inferiour quality, in remembrance of her Humble LORD, now exalted. And it is more than probable that fhe was prefent with the *Apoftles*, when the HOLY GHOST came upon them, and that fhe there received the *firft* Fruits of the SPIRIT. After which time we reade no more of her in *Holy Writ*. For where, and with whom, how ftrictly, and how pioufly, fhe liv'd after the Afcention of CHRIST, till the houre of her death, faith *Idelphonfus*, is onely knowne to GOD, the fearcher of hearts; and to the *Angels*, her diligent Vifiters. The reafon which many alledge, why neither the reft of her

Acts i. 14, 1.

* *S. Bernhard. In ferm. de verb. Apocalyp. Signum magnū.*

Idelphonfus. Serm. 5. de Affump. Virg.

life, nor death are penned by the Holy *Evangelists* is this, that the *Apostles* were so busied about the Conversion of the *Iewes* and the *Gentiles*, & enlarging of the *Christian Church*, that they had no time to set downe the particular Acts of her life, after her SONNES Ascention, nor the severall Circumstances of her death, as where, when, and how she dyed. Some *Authours* peremptorily maintaine (upon what ground I know not) that she liv'd to her *seaventieth yeare*, and to her last houre dwelt in *Ierusalem*, neare to her SONNES Sepulchre. Others upon no better warrant, averre that she went with *Iohn* into *Asia*, and continued with him at *Ephesus* till her death; and urge the authority of *Ignatius*, who affirmes that she wrote to him in these words, " *I will come with* Iohn *to see thee, and thy friends, &c.*" Concerning her death, some avouch that the *Apostles*, and the most eminent of the *Primitive Church*, were present at it. *Damascen* saith that CHRIST was also there in Person, and that He thus spake to her: " ' *Come My Blessed*

Damascen. ser. de dormit. Virg.

S. Ignatius.

Damascen. Serm. de dormit. Virg.

"' Mother *into the rest I have prepar'd for thee;*' and that shee thus in way of answer prayed to Him: 'Into Thy Hands, O my SONNE, I commend my Spirit: Receive that deare Soule which Thou hast preserved free from all rebuke.'"
As I will not justifie all these their Assertions for true; so, on the other side, I will not condemne them as erroneous, not being able to convince them of untruth; and for ought I know, they may have pass'd by unwritten Tradition from man to man. I will therefore affirmatively say nothing but this, that most assuredly her death was welcome to her, in that she had so often both meditated and practised it, having many times by Austerity, and Contemplation, departed this life ere she left it. If that of *Seneca* be true, that to dye well, is to dye willingly, then certainly she dyed the death of the Righteous. She was not ignorant that Death to the just is no other than a delivery from prison; a laying downe of a burthen; the end of a Pilgrimage; the unmanacling of the Soule; the discharging of a due debt to

[marginal note: Seneca.]

Nature; the returne into our true Country; the dore that opens into a never fading Life; the entrance into the celestiall *Kingdome;* and the Vsher that was to conduct her to her Blessed Saviour, with Whom she had mentally conversed ever since He left the earth: Since which time there be who avouch that she never willingly saw any man.

HER ASSUMPTION.

HE same modesty I have shew'd in treating of her Death, I shall reserve in discoursing of her Assumption; which by many of the *Fathers*, all of the *Romish Church*, and some of the *Reformed*, is held for an undoubted Truth, though upon no sounder proofes than the former produce concerning her departure hence. *Bullinger* directly backs this opinion. "*We doe beleeve*," saith he, "*that the Wombe of the* God*-Bearing Virgin, and the Temple of the* Holy Ghost, *that is, her Sacred Body, to have beene assumed into* Heaven." *Brentius* leaves it indifferent to us to beleeve whether or no she ascended in Soule, in body, or both.

<small>Bullinger.
Lib. de origine erroris, cap. 16.</small>

<small>Brentius.</small>

Assumpta est Maria in cælum;
gaudet exercitus angelorum. Alleluia.

HER ASSUMPTION.

THE same modesty I ha[ve] shew'd in treating of [her] D[ea]th, I shall reserve in [disco]ursing of her Assumptio[n, whi]ch by [m]any of the *Fathers*, all of th[e Catholique Chu]rch, and some of the *Refor[med] h[old fo]r an undoubted Truth, thoug[h groundded] upon [le]sser proofes than the forme[r di]s[cours]e concerning her departure hen[ce.] [Bul]linger directly backs this opinion[. "]*We doe beleeve*," saith he, "*that th[e] Wombe of the* GOD-Bearing Virg[in, and] *the Temple of the* HOLY GHOST, *that is [her] Sacred Body, to have been [assumed] into* Heaven." *Brentius* [saith it is in]different to us to beleeve w[hethe]r no[t] she ascended in Soule, in bod[y, or bo]th.

B[ull]inger. L[ib.] de origine err[or.] [ca]p. 16.

[Bren]tius.

Assumpta est Maria in cœlum;
gaudet exercitus angelorum. Alleluia.

Her Assumption.

"*It might well be,*" saith he, "*that as Enoch was translated in body into* Heaven, *and as many bodies of the* Saints *did rise with* Christ; *so* Mary *also might in body be assumed into* Heaven. *But most certain it is that she obtained everlasting Felicity.*" And some ther be who demand why God might not manifest His Power by her, privy to so many Divine Secrets, and Mysteries, as well as by an *Angell*, or as by *Elias*, who after long prayer, was taken up in a Fiery Chariot. Some againe, (who hold that the Dead who arose with Christ, ascended with Him into Glory, and were not againe reduc't into Ashes) thinke the Assumption of *Mary* altogether as likely.

Damascen saith, "*the Workes of the* Deity *are therefore possible, because Omnipotent; and that there are some things, which though they are wholly omitted in* Holy Scriptures, *yet upon evident reasons they are believ'd;*" and exemplifies his position in the Assumption of the *Virgin Mary*. *Dammianus* argues thus; "*That as conceiving without sinne,*

Homil. 1. in Die Assump. Virgin. *See* Athanasius *on this very point, a Father of great repute, both with the* Latines *and the* Greekes *in his serm.* in Evang. de sanctissima Deipara. *And* Iohannes Rivius *in his Booke* de abusibus Ecclesiæ *though hee dares not maintaine her corporal Assumption; yet hee will not deny it, as being a thing probable enough.*
Damascen.

Dammianus.

"shee brought forth her Sonne without paine, a curse laid on all other women: so might it well be that shee who was without sinne, might overcome Death, the reward of it." Some goe about to prove it by the Text, "*Arise* Lord *into thy rest, thou, and the* Arke *of thy Sanctification.*" Nay, I have read a moderne *Oratour*, who thus elegantly describes the manner of it: "*When*," saith hee, "*the Soule of this Sweet* One, *reactuated her body, she arose in Triumph from her Sepulcher, and was assumed into* Heaven. *In her passage thither, the* Orbes *bowed, and bended themselves to make her a triumphant Arch through which shee might passe in greater state. The* Sunne, *with his brightest Beames, imbrac't her, that it might be said,* A woman was cloath'd with the Sunne. *The* Moone *stooped to her, that it might be divulg'd the* Moone *was under her feet. The brightest of the* Starres *interwove themselves to make her a radiant Crowne, &c.*" But this description is no more Theologicall, than the consent of the Orbes is Philosophicall;

Ps. cxxxii. 8.

Her Assumption.

and is no way correspondent to the dignity of our Sacred *Subject*, on whose triumphant Entry into *Heaven*, having beene a faithfull, and reverent Attender, I will now returne to vindicate her Honour here on *Earth*, and make an Apology to *Christians* (with shame, and horrour I speake it) for CHRISTS Owne *Mother*.

THE AUTHORS APOLOGY FOR CHRISTS OWN MOTHER.

T may pleafe then the gentle *Reader*, to underftand that *two* Queftions arife amongft the Moderne *Divines.* The *one* whether or no fhe merited to be the *Mother* of GOD; the *other* which way fhe could deferve that greateft of Glories. For the *firft*, they affirm that never any Creature merited fo great a bleffing as the Incarnation of GODS OWNE SONNE. For He fent, fay they, His SONNE into the world, not urg'd thereto by our merits, but out of His Owne meere Grace and Goodneffe. It was a worke of His Charity, and Condefcending, not of Retribution, or Obligation: and therefore that

he chose not the *Virgin Mary* to be the *Mother* of CHRIST, as she was a *Virgin*, humble, obedient, adorn'd with Faith, Charity, and other Divine Vertues; but because GOD had decreed her to beare His Onely SONNE, therefore His best Pleasure was, she should be *Mistresse* of Perfections, suteable to so high a Calling. Wherfore *Saint Paul* saies; "Because GOD "hath predestinated us, therefore He calles, "justifies, and glorifies us," and not because we are just, therefore He electeth us. [Rom. viii. 30.]

Againe, they argue thus; that all our merits depend on CHRIST, and are deriv'd from Him, and therefore she was without all desert before her SONNE had imparted it to her. That this was well knowne to her, is manifestly proved by her Divine Hymne, in which she acknowledgeth all good to proceed from Him; and therefore to Him ascribeth all Honour and Glory. Others her Champions, who couragiously fight, not onely for her Heavenly, but earthly Triumph, confesse that she was not prefer'd to that supreme Dignity by Desert, but by Congruity, as they call it: that is, not that she was absolutely worthy of so great a Grace, but that since GOD had fixed a decree to send His dearely beloved SONNE amongst us, she of all others was the fittest to conceive, and beare Him.

But here againe they differ about the way, in that so many waies they hold her capable of this inestimable Diadem. Some give the preheminency to her Virginity, and say, the love of that drew the SONNE out of the Bosome of His FATHER, into her hallowed Wombe; and therefore the Text saies not, that a Faithfull, an Obedient, or an Humble shall conceive, but a *Virgin*. Others attribute this supreme Favour to her Faith, by which (as *Saint Paul* demonstrates) all the Miraculous Workes of the *Old Testament* have beene begunne and perfected: Wherefore her *Cousin Elizabeth* said to her, "Blessed art "thou, because thou hast beleeved." Some ascribe this infinite Honour done her, to her Humility, to which all other Vertues flow, no otherwise than the waters naturally runne to the lowest places. This

S. Elizabeth.

caus'd her to say in her gratefull Hymne, "*Thou hast regarded the lowlinesse of thy* "Hand-maid." Others impute the conferring of this greatest Blessing on her, to her Obedience, in that she committed all to the Will of the Highest, with this Protestation, "*Behold the* Hand-maid *of* "*the* Lord, *be it to mee according to Thy* "*Word.*" Others give her Charity the uper hand, which, (as *Saint Paul* testifies) gives life and Spirit to all other Vertues, they being without it no other than dead Images. Lastly, some there are who will not award the Crowne to this or that peculiar Vertue residing in her, but to the united Harmony of them altogether; for they say, it is not this string, or that, makes the Musicke, but the accord, and consent of all. For my owne part, (Divinity not being the spheare wherein my studies move) a modest Inquisition will better become me, than a bold and peremptory Conclusion in any point of Controversie. Wherfore I most humbly submit this, and all things else Divine, by me handled, to the Censure and Deter-

<small>S. Mary.</small>

<small>S. Mary.</small>

mination of the *Church* of *England*, whose not Connivence alone, but Approbation I know I shall have, in boldly affirming that she was a Transcendent *Creature*, not to be ranked in respect of her Worth, with any of her sexe, but to have a place assign'd her apart, and above them all; being not to be considered as a meere *Woman*, but as a *Type*, or an *Idæa* of an Accomplisht Piety.

They who uphold the latter of the aforesaid opinions, erre not so much, in my judgement, in the adoring extreame, as some too severe maintainers of the former doe, in the neglecting. They are so farre from praising her themselves, that they most unjustly deprive her of the Praise given her by others. The *Puritans* in generall, but especially the obstinate *Non-Conformists* of this *Land*, are those I meane, who as in their course Oratory they called *Queene Elizabeth*, *Queene Besse*, so they give this *Holy Virgin* no higher a Stile, than of *Mal, Gods *Maide*. They reject all Testimonies of her Worth, as *Haile*, Mary, *Full of Grace*; *The* Lord *is*

---

* *I have both heard these irreverent speeches, and read them censurd* *with thee*; and, *Thou haſt found Grace with* God; and, *Hee that is Mighty, hath magnified mee*; and *All generations ſhall call mee* Bleſſed; and, *Bleſſed is the Wombe that bore Thee*; and *Bleſſed are the Paps that gave Thee ſucke*; and *whence comes this that the* Mother *of my* Lord *ſhould come to me?* and, *Bleſſed art thou amongſt women*; and, *Bleſſed is the* Fruit *of thy Wombe.* They abhorre to heare her call'd *Domina*, *Lady*, or *Deipara*, God-*Bearing*, few of them being ſo learned, even in their owne Faculty, as to know that they who ſo ſtile her, thinke not that the God-Head proceeds from her, but that ſhe brought forth Christ, in Whom was the Union of Both Natures; and therefore, they being inſeparable, ſhe muſt by ſtrong conſequence be deliver'd of both God and Man. And why are they deterr'd from giving her theſe honourable *Epithites?* Becauſe forſooth they challenge to themſelves a greater meaſure of knowledge, but a leſſer of Piety, than did their Anceſtors. By diſclaiming words, and phraſes familiar to Antiquity, and by

in a Manuſcript of a moſt learned Doctour of the Engliſh Church. And this is very credible to al ſuch as beare and peruſe their illiterate Sermons, full of invectives againſt the antient Saints, and Fathers of the Church; and abounding with predications of their owne ignorant Brethren.

inventing new, lesse reverent, and significant; they give all men to understand that they had rather be reputed **good** *Grammarians*, than *Christians*; and had rather give Names to the *Church*, than accept them from her; and cherish prophane Novelties, rather than allow of Reverent Antiquities. They wrest many places of *Scripture* to prove that CHRIST Himselfe slighted and rebuked her, which depravations of theirs (were my *Readers Turkes*) I would draw into the Light and lay their deformity open to all; but it is needlesse (I trust) to informe a *Christian*, that He Who hath said, *Honour thy Father and thy Mother*, would surely never breake His Owne Commandement; and by slighting His *Mother*, trench upon a sinne of all others most detestable in His Sight, Ingratitude. Of one thing I will assure them, till they are good *Marians*, they shall never be good *Christians*; while they derogate from the dignity of the *Mother*, they cannot truely honour the SONNE. They are, I confesse, much more favourable to her, than the *Iewes*, but by farre more detracting from her than the *Turkes*; which Affertion of mine is ftrengthened with evident proofes both out of the *Iewifh Thalmud*, and *Turkifh Alchoran*. The *Iewes* call her *Thlua*, as much as to fay, *Butchereffe*, or the *Wife* of a Butcher; and *Sono*, a publike Sinner; and *Thmea*, one polluted with all manner of uncleane and filthy luft. And all of their *Religion* are enjoyned in folemne Prayer made in their *Sinagogues* thrice every *day* to curfe CHRIST, His *Mother*, and all the *Chriftian Sect*; as is to be found at large, in the *third Booke* of the *Thalmud*, wholly compos'd of ridiculous fables, groffe errors, and horrid blafphemies. True it is, that the *Turkifh Alchoran* now acknowledgeth CHRIST to be GOD, and now againe denies Him; taking Him in at the fore-dore, and fhutting Him out at the backe; yet doe they hold Him the greateft of *Prophets*, next their *Mahomet*. But His *Mother* they magnifie above all women that ever breathed this ayre. Let us heare this Oracle fpeake, in all things elfe falfe, but in this moft

The Iewifh Thalmud.

The Turkifh Alchoran.

true. These ensuing are the very formall words of the *Alchoran:* "O Mary, excel‑ lent above all men and women, who per‑ severest in the study of GOD Onely." And in another place; "O Mary, GOD hath chosen thee, and purified thee; Hee hath elected thee to make thee famous above the women of all Ages:" and againe; "Mary by behaving her selfe wisely, is guilty neither of malice, nor any wickednesse, which caused us to breath our soule into her." Lastly, "that many men have beene perfect; but no woman was ever found perfect, but Mary the Mother of IESUS." But though Truth is to be imbrac't where ever we finde it, yet it will appeare more gracefull in the mouthes of *Christians,* whose most learned, most eloquent, and most judicious *Doctour,* we will produce, giving this Testimony of this our dearest *Lady.* "Except (saith he) the Holy Virgin Mary, (whom for the Honour I owe my LORD and MASTER, I will not name when sinne is my subject) whom to have had Grace infus'd into her, wholly to subdue sinne, wee know

Marginal notes:
The Al‑choran.
Againe.
And againe.
Lastly.
S. Austin lib. de nat. & grat. cap. 36.

"by this, that shee was thought worthy to
"conceive and bring forth Him, Who as-
"suredly was without sinne: *This* Virgin,
"*I say, excepted, if we could recall, and*
"*assemble together all the* Saints *departed,*
"*and should aske them, if they were with-*
"*out sinne, they would unanimously thus*
"*answere:* 'If we should say we have no
"'sinne, we deceive our selves, and there is
"'no truth in us.'" But because the
Fathers are no way suspected of neglect
towards her, we will spare their Verdicts,
and chiefly insert their Commendations of
her, who were the first *Reformers* of our
Church. *Luther* shall be their Leader,
who saith, "That none but the Virgin   Luther.
"Mary *either was, or ever shall be so Holy:*
"*That the* FRUIT *of her Wombe shall be*
"*Blessed, since no other conceives without*
"*pleasure and sinne:*" and againe; "*In*   Againe.
"this is Mary *Blessed, That so great Gifts*
"*are given to her, as surpasse humane un-*
"*derstanding. For hence all Honour and*
"*Beatitude proceeds, that in the vniversall*
"*humane Race one Person should be supe-*
"*riour to the rest, to whom none should be*

Life of the Blessed Virgin:

"equall, because *One and the Same* SONNE is common to her with the Heavenly FA- THER." This he applyes to that saying of *Mary*, "*Hee that is Mighty hath mag- nified mee*," &c. The same *Author* in another place sayes; "*Mary is our Mo- ther*, CHRIST *our* BROTHER, *and* GOD *our* FATHER, *and that all this is true, the* Faithfull *by effect doe finde*." *Calvin* cals her his *Mistresse*. "*Wee willingly (saith he) take* Mary *for our* Mistresse, *to whose Doctrine and Precepts we are obe- dient*." *Erasmus stiles her his *Savior- esse*. *Occolampadius* thus delivers his ap- probation of her: "*I trust in* GOD *it shall never be said of me, that I did oppose the dignity of* Mary, *towards whom to be never so little ill affected, I hold to be a most certaine signe of a re- probate minde. She who is above all, Queene of all, whom* GOD, *above all, hath honoured, should not she be esteemed amongst all the most eminent?*" *Bucerus* protesteth; "*That a Godly minde will not judge, but charitably, and piously of her, who brought forth* CHRIST *our* LORD."

Againe.

Once more.

Calvin.

* *Thob Erasmus was not a Reformer of our Church, yet he is much sus- pected by the Romish Church, and most service- able to the Protestant in the setting out of the Fathers.*

Occolampa- dius.

Bucerus.

Bullingerus concludes; "*If* Mary *be Blessed amongst all women, and to bee pronounced* Blessed *by all* Nations, *most cursed are the* Iewes, *who never cease to revile and slander her; and most unhappy are those Counterfeit* Christians, *who (being little better than* Iewes) *robbe her of the praise due to her. Needs must shee be indued with a singular, most select, and perpetuall Virginity and Purity, who is especially chosen by* GOD *to be the* Temple *of his* SONNE, *and the* Mother *of the* MOST HOLY." Now if any of these contradict themselves by pulling downe in other places those Trophies of her Praise, which here they have erected, they are to be answered as the Satyre did the Man with whom he said he would no longer converse, because he saw hot and cold breath to issue from the same mouth.

But to leave them; all parts of the world have produced Admirers of her Worth:—*Syria* hath brought forth *Ephraim*: *Antiochia*; *Saint Chrysostome*: *Capadocia*; *Saint Basill*, and *Saint Nazianzen*: *Constantinople*; *Germanus*, and *Proclus*:

Dalmatia; *Saint Hierome*: *Germany*; *Rupertus*, *Albertus*, and *Agrippa*: *England*; *Bæda*: *France*; *Bernhard*: *Spaine*; *Alphonsus*: *Italy*; *Aquinas*, and *Bonauenture*: *Affrick*; *Saint Cyprian*, and *Saint Austin*: *Greece*; *Dionysius Areopagita*, &c.

To these succeed famous *Christian Poets*, Antient and Moderne, who have written *Pannegyricks* upon her, as *Bæda*: *Gregorius Nazianzenus*: *Innocentius Pontifex*: *Actius Sanazarius*: *Adam de Sancto Victore*: *Alcimus Avitus*: *Antonius Muretus*: *Aurelius Prudentius*: *Baptista Mantuanus*: *Claudianus*: *Franciscus Petrarcha*: *Godfridus Viterbiensis*: *Hieronymus Vida*: *Paulinus*: *D. Philippus Menzelius*: *Rudolphus Agricola*: *Sedulius*: *Venantius Fortunatus*, &c.

To these I adde many *Emperours*, *Princes*, and *Princesses*, and a world of devout Great Ones, who have beene her professed Admirers, as *Constantine* the *Great*; *Charles* the *Great*; *Pulcheria Augusta*; *Henry* the *Second*, *Emperour*; *Alphonsus the Chaste*, in *Spaine*; *Edovar-*

dus, in *Hungarie*; *Bolislaus*, in *Polonia*; *Venceslaus*, in *Bohemia*.

All which are Canonized for *Saints*, and have erected and dedicated Temples to her Memory. Neither have the *Princes* of this our *Ile* beene defective in doing her all possible Honour, and in Consecrating Chappels, and Temples to her Memory. *Fredericke* the *Third Emperour*, made the Contemplation of her, almost his onely food. *Stephanus, King* of *Hungarie,* called his *Kingdome* the *Marian Family*. In this glorious Family, whole *Kingdomes* and *Common-wealths* have enrolled themselves. My Arithmeticke will not serve mee to number all those who have Registred their names in the *Sodalitie* of the *Rosary* of this our *Blessed Lady;* the Originall of which is derived from the Battaile of *Naupactun*, gain'd by *Iohn* of *Austria*, and the *Christians*, which Victory was attributed to her Intercession with her Sonne. The *Colonian Sodallity* first instituted, had out of *Lovaine*, 4000. out of *Brabant*, 30000. out of *Gueldria*, 4000. out of *Holland* and *Zeland*, 7000. &c.

Many *Holy Orders* alfo are of this *Sodality*, as the *Benedictines*, the *Ciftertians*, the *Francifcans*, the *Carthufians*, and many others. If all thefe Teftimonies and Examples of great, worthy, and pious people, will not move us to honour her; we fhall be judg'd both unworthy of this life, and ignorant of that better to come. For fhame, let not us alone deny her that Honour, and Praife which all the world allowes her.

After thefe impartiall Witneffes of her Worth, we will place thofe divine Priviledges imparted to her by the ALMIGHTY, for which we have (if that alone were fufficient) the Authority of many pious, learned men.

1 Priviledge.   *Firft*, they affirme, that her chafte eyes fent forth fuch Divine Beames, that (though her Lovelineffe moved not onely all mindes to honour her, and all eyes to gaze on hers) yet they never kindled an unholy fire in the moft Adulterate bofome. A facred Priviledge, peculiar to this *Saint* alone; for it was the will of her Omnipotent SONNE, that neither *Sathan* nor his *Ministers* should conspire the overthrow of that chiefe *Temple* of His SPIRIT, which His Flesh had inhabited so long; nor any impure thought ayme at the mudding of this purest *Fountaine*. Whether her Prophetick Soule foresaw the snares of the ungodly, and so shun'd them, they say not; once for certaine they averre, that Temptations aym'd at her, broke like Haile against a Rocke; nor could all the Engines of the world, the flesh, and the Divell hurt her more, then can the vapours arising from the earth, reach the holy Inhabitants of *Heaven*. And this opinion (for ought I know, I submit it to better Judgements) may without, or profanation, or blasphemy, be admitted into all honest bosomes: for if, beyond the power of Nature, He preserved *Ionas* entire in the *Whales* Belly; if He protected *Daniel* from the ravenous *Lyons*; should not He secure her from Corruption, whom he had adorn'd with so many Vertues and Dignities?

Next, they hold, that she was not onely without blemish, but her very lookes sent

2 *Priviledge.*

forth such Heavenly Rayes; that whosoever beheld them, drew thence a Vestall Fire that never went out, and vowed an everlasting Virginity. If this be a Truth, it is a curious one; and it is not materiall at all, whether or no it be beleeved, or rejected.

3 Priviledge. *Thirdly*, that she conceiv'd and bore her SONNE, not onely without paine (the common curse annexed to Childe-bearing), but with infinite delight. This also is a Curiosity; and of no importance whether it be swallowed or no.

4 Priviledge. *Fourthly*, and *lastly*, that she had a frigidity of Soule, which quencht in her, all heat of carnall concupiscence. This *last* priviledge is implyed in the *first;* and may perchance safely be received. The truth is, we may securely give her all humane Attributes (not encroaching on the Divine) for she was in dignity above all, but GOD Himselfe. Faith, and Charity, the fulnesse of the Law, were in her at full. She was in an active, and contemplative life, admirable. The tongue, esteemed the worst part in a woman, was in her the best; which well might charme eares; offend them, it could not. Her Soule weigh'd her Conceptions, and gave them a rayment of Vertues owne hiew; for certainly so cleere thoughts were apparell'd, in as faire words. She who both after her Conception, and at other times, is commended to us by the *Sacred Scriptures*, for laying up all Holy Sayings in her heart, can we imagine that she could speake amisse? Neither could she commit ahy undecent act, who liv'd in a Light to others inaccessible. They who maintaine that for a time the whole *Militant Church* was in her alone, have probability to backe them; for I know not in whom else it could remaine, when his *Apostles, Disciples, Friends, Kindred*, and all others forsooke CHRIST, she onely excepted, who would not leave Him, Who from before His Birth, had stucke to her. I will conclude with this Assertion: That if ever the Soule of any mortall enjoyed here on earth, the embraces of her Heavenly SPOUSE, and tooke from Him a kisse, sweeter than all the Easterne Odours, this was she.

APOSTROPHE AUTHORIS.

ND here, O Blessed Virgin!
" *I leave to discourse further*
" *of thee, and direct my speech*
" *to thee.* O thou Eternall
" Glory *of thy Sexe!* had the Queene *of*
" Sheba *seene thee, as she did* Salomon,
" *shee had not so soone beene delivered out*
" *of the Trance into which her Admiration*
" *cast her. In thee shee might have dis-*
" *covered all the perfections of which wo-*
" *man kinde is capable, who wer't indeed*
" *vertually thy Sexe. In thee* Aspatia *might*
" *have found her Modesty;* Livia, *her*
" *Prudency;* Sulpitia, *her Majestie and*
" *Gravity;* Cornelia, *her Patience;* Lu-
" cretia, *her Chastity;* Porcia, *her Forti-*
" *tude;* Tanaquill, *her Industry;* Plau-

"tina, *her Frugality; and all these in*
"*eminency. But why talke I of the* Hea-
"then *to thee, who didst not onely outstrip*
"*in manifold Vertues all the* Femall, *but*
"*the* Masculine Saints *themselves? Thou*
"*didst excell* Abel *in Innocency;* Abra-
"ham, *in Faith;* Isaac, *in Obedience;*
"David, *in Gentlenesse; the* Prophets *and*
"Apostles, *in Piety; and the* Martyrs, *in*
"Patience. *O thou whom* Heaven *would*
"*have of the same Constancy, Purity, and*
"*Sublimity with it selfe, thou art so farre*
"*from having an equall, that all thy sexe*
"*cannot afford a worthy witnesse of thy*
"Excellencies! *O thou* Mother *of the true*
"Moses, *who never put on the yoke of*
"Pharaoh, *but stood free in the middest of*
"Egypt! *Thou* Rodde *of* Iesse, *alwaies*
"*straight, who broughtst forth the* Fruit
"*of Life! thou wert here a terrestriall*
"Paradice, *whereinto* Serpent *never en-*
"*tred; on which* Gods *malediction was*
"*never impos'd; and hast no doubt, now*
"*in the Cælestiall* Paradice *a conspicuous*
"*seate above all the* Angelicall Orders,
"*and next thy Glorifi'd* Sonne *Himselfe.*

" For if CHRIST *Promise to all His fellow*
" *feeling Members, that if they suffer with*
" *Him, they shall raigne with Him; if*
" *they dye with Him, they shall live with*
" *Him; what eminent place in* Heaven
" *shalt thou have assigned thee, who in*
" *Soule didst suffer for Him more, than all*
" *His* Martyrs? *O thou bashfull* Morne
" *that didst precede and produce our* SUNNE!
" *Thou* Circumscription (*if I may so say*)
" *of the* UNCIRCUMSCRIBED! *Thou* Roote
" *to this* HERBE *of Grace! Thou* Mother
" *of our* CREATOUR! *Thou* Nurse *to Him*
" *by Whom all things are fed! Thou* Com-
" prehender *of the* INCOMPREHENSIBLE!
" *Thou* Bearer *of Him Whose Word sus-*
" *taines the* Globes! *Thou who didst im-*
" *part Flesh to Him, Who wanted nothing*
" *else! Thou* Sarah, *thou* Mother *of many*
" Nations, *who broughtst forth our* Isaac,
" *our* LAUGHTER, *when a just Sorrow con-*
" *ceiv'd for a losse esteem'd irreparable had*
" *clouded this inferiour World! O pardon,*
" Gratious Princesse, *my weake endeavours*
" *to summe up thy Value, which come as*
" *short of thee, as my head does of* Heaven.

Apostrophe Authoris.

" *Nothing that is not it selfe glorified, can
" expresse thy Glory to the height. Thou
" deserv'st a Quire of* Queenes *here, and
" another of* Angels *in* Heaven *to sing thy
" Praises. Were all the* Earths Brood,
" *the* Droppes, *the* Sands *of the* Sea, *and
" the* Starres *of* Heaven *tongued, they could
" not all expresse thee so well, as a silent
" Extasie. I confesse, O my Sweetest* Lady!
" *that now I have said all I can of thee, I
" have but done like* Timanthes, *a great
" Master in his Art, who being to expresse
" the vastnesse of a* Cyclops *in a small ta-
" ble, drew onely his Thumbe, by which the
" spectators might judge of his large pro-
" portion. To give thee an estimation an-
" swerable to thy Merit, is a thing impos-
" sible. I must therefore be content to doe
" by thee, as the antient* Heathen *did by the
" Images of their* Gods; *on whose heads,
" when by reason of their height, they could
" not place the Crownes, offer'd to their
" Deities, they humbly layd them at their
" feet.*"

FINIS.

LONDON:

Printed by *Thomas Harper*, for *Iohn Waterson*, and are to be sold at his Shop in *Pauls Church Yard*, at the Signe of the Crowne. 1635.

Reprinted by *Whittingham* and *Wilkins*, at the Chiswick Press, 21, Tooks Court, Chancery Lane, for *Edward Lumley*, and sold by him at his Shop in *Oxford Street*.
1860.

www.ingramcontent.com/pod-product-compliance
Lightning Source LLC
Chambersburg PA
CBHW022103230426
43672CB00008B/1266